Meet St Paul

By the same author

Matthew Lays It on the Line!

Luke's Case for Christianity

The Bible Reading Fellowship was founded 'to encourage the systematic and intelligent reading of the Bible, to emphasize its spiritual message and to take advantage of new light shed on Holy Scripture'.

Over the years the Fellowship has proved a trustworthy guide for those who want an open, informed and contemporary approach to the Bible. It retains a sense of the unique authority of Scripture as a prime means by which God communicates.

As an ecumenical organization, the Fellowship embraces all Christian traditions and its readers are to be found in most parts of the world.

Meet St Paul

An introduction to the man,
his achievement and his correspondence

Reginald White

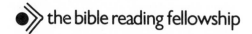 the bible reading fellowship

The Bible Reading Fellowship
Warwick House
25 Buckingham Palace Road
London SW1W 0PP

First published 1989
© BRF 1989

British Library CIP data
White, R. E. O. (Reginald Ernest Oscar), *1914–*
    Meet Saint Paul.
    1. Bible N.T. Paul, the Apostle, Saint
    I. Title
    225.9'24
    ISBN 0-90016482-4

Filmset by Eta Services (Typesetters) Ltd, Beccles, Suffolk
Printed in Great Britain at the
University Press, Cambridge

CONTENTS

The basis of this study is the Revised Standard Version (RSV) except where
the New International Version (NIV), the New English Version (NEB), the
Authorised (King James') Version (AV/KJV) or the United Bible Societies'
Greek Testament, are occasionally consulted.

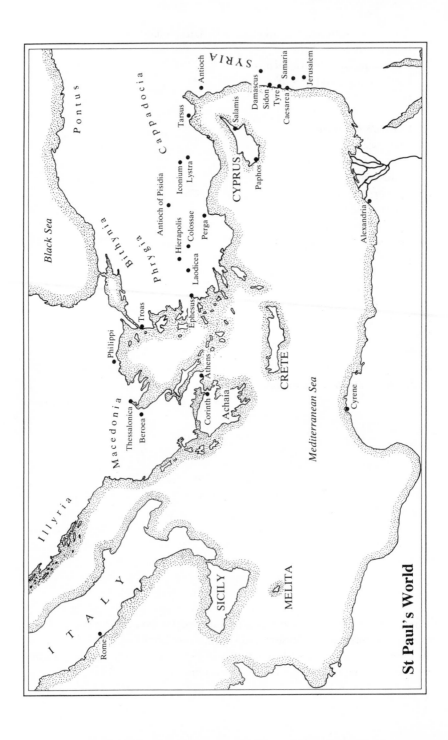

St Paul's World

CHAPTER 1

A Living Miracle

Preparatory Reading: Acts 9:1–19, 26:1–20, Romans 1:16–32,
2 Corinthians 4:7–12, 10:1–10

A living miracle was certainly how Paul appeared to Christians who first met him after his conversion. Everything about the man was unexpected and inexplicable, suspicious or just wonderful. The Christian to whom he was sent for initial counselling could not believe his ears: 'But Lord,' Ananias protested, 'I have heard from many about this man, how much evil he has done...' And the church Paul sought to join on his return to Jerusalem refused to believe that he could be a disciple, until generous Barnabas stood guarantor for Paul's sincerity and brought him into fellowship.

The Christians were right to be cautious. Paul had gone out a persecutor, 'in raging fury... breathing threats and murder'; and had returned a convert. His conversion could have been a ruse to gain information for further repression. The conversion of a truly religious man, as distinct from a godless one, is rare, and Paul was a convinced and zealous Judaist. For him to become a Christian involved rethinking his deepest beliefs, overcoming his most cherished feelings, admitting he had been disastrously wrong. All that he had previously held sacred must now be counted worthless. Nothing in the church's experience prepared it to expect so radical a change in such a man.

Besides, the circumstances were so improbable. To win this man, it seemed, Christ was his own evangelist. Riding into Damascus almost alone, without apostle to instruct him or congregation to woo him, Paul encountered (so he said, speaking of a 'heavenly vision') the risen Christ, probably some three years after the resurrection. Jesus spoke to him, called his name, reproached him, and took charge of his life. 'I was apprehended,' Paul says.

Such direct divine encounter created a new dimension of experience, and Paul's response, 'Who are you, *Lord*...? What shall I do, *Lord?*' set a wholly new pattern for the future. That was Paul's story, but could it be true?

We owe the story to Luke, the cultivated Gentile doctor, once a convert to Judaism but later a Christian, whom Paul met at Troas about AD 50 (or possibly a little earlier, at Antioch in Syria). Luke became Paul's constant travelling companion, except for the brief period when he was left to nurture the infant church at Philippi. He kept a journal of his travels, and wherever possible he enquired of first-generation Christians for details of the life of Jesus, especially during his two years spent at Jerusalem, AD 57–59 (Luke 1:1–4). From his gospel and his *Acts of the Apostles* it can be shown that Luke was a skilled, observant, careful writer, with excellent qualifications and abundant opportunities to learn of Paul's earlier years, from other Christians as well as from Paul himself.

Though strongly attached to Paul, Luke shows a very independent mind: his thought and style reveal surprisingly few traces of his long companionship with the strong-minded apostle. We are, therefore, privileged to possess two sources of information about Paul — Luke's *Acts*, and Paul's own correspondence. This must be remembered as we strive to see Paul through Luke's eyes as well as his own. It explains differences that otherwise would puzzle us.

To cite only two examples: At the beginning of his missionary career Paul was painfully involved in controversies over Judaist scruples about welcoming Gentiles into the church on the ground of their faith alone. Paul's earliest writings show his depth of feeling over this issue. But by the time Luke met Paul, a church council had pronounced upon the question, and the heat had died from these disagreements — though parties of 'Judaist Christians' continued to harass Paul from time to time.

By then, too, Paul's own understanding of his missionary task had deepened with experience. Thus Luke was far more aware of Paul's vision of the universal church than of his earlier inter-Jewish problems. As a Gentile himself, Luke may not have known, or may not have sympathized with, the theological subtleties by which Paul sought to reconcile that universalist vision with his inherited belief in Israel's special election.

So, too, with the two accounts of Paul's teaching. Luke records Paul's preaching to Jewish audiences in the synagogues and to pagan hearers in market places, on Mar's Hill at Athens, in a lecture hall at Ephesus, offering the elementary gospel to first-time hearers. Paul's letters, on the other hand, were sent to Christian churches, of varying maturity and facing varying problems. It is hardly surprising that the two versions of Paul's teaching reflect different situations and emphases. If they did not, we would suspect Luke of making up Paul's speeches from his correspondence!

And so it is with the varying accounts of this astonishing story of Paul's conversion. Luke doubtless first heard it privately, from Paul's own lips, as Paul explained himself and his mission to his new friend. Luke heard it again as Paul told it from the stair of the barracks at the corner of the temple courtyard in Jerusalem, to a hostile crowd that cried, 'Away with him!' Luke heard the story yet again, presented more fully, and defensively, with legal formality, before king Agrippa in the governor's court at Caesarea. Meanwhile Paul had already unveiled his own inmost thoughts about it in his early letter to Galatia; and he explained himself once again in a letter to the church at Rome.

We are able, in this way, to see the event from varying angles, and with full knowledge of all that followed from it. But Paul's first contemporaries knew nothing of his deep disappointment with Judaism, of his struggles and failures, and his growing conviction that while the sacred law engendered a sense of sin it could do nothing to transform man's nature and set him free.

Later they would learn how even his prayers were haunted by the memory that he had consented to Stephen's assassination (Acts 22:19–20). His public speeches, also, sometimes referred in deep penitence to his persecuting days. Towards the end of his life Paul still testifies to the effect of the courage of the persecuted upon the conscience of the persecutor (Philippians 1:27–28). So Paul rode to Damascus in mental turmoil, 'kicking' like an angry ox against the 'goads' of doubt, disappointment and guilt, the violence of his persecuting zeal itself evidence of the storm and uncertainty within him.

Even so, the dramatic change in his experience, character, and life style was no less miraculous to Paul himself. He always speaks of conversion as a direct intervention of God into human experience, a new creation, when God again says 'Let there be light' — a new beginning of life; a resurrection out of spiritual death to new life in Christ. Conversion is a spiritual parallel to the exodus of Israel from Egypt, transferring the soul from the dominion of darkness into the kingdom of God's Son. Thus Paul, too, saw himself now, 'in Christ', as a living miracle of divine mercy and power.

But to others, a conversion so unprecedented could only be made credible by the quality of the life that followed. Long afterwards, the event could be seen as the 'display' of Christ's patience, an example for all time of the saving power of Christ (1 Timothy 1:16); and partly for this reason, alone among the many thousands of conversions that enrich the story of the church, Paul's first surrender to Christ is marked in the Christian calendar by a festival of its own (25 January).

Strength in Weakness

The first evidence which the church received of the reality of Paul's conversion lay in his amazing evangelizing zeal and success. Already at Damascus he publicly declared his new-found faith, and before long news reached Palestine Christians of congregations springing up in Cyprus, Pamphylia, at Lystra, Iconium, Derbe, Troas, and Ephesus in Asia Minor, at Philippi, Thessalonica, Beroea, Athens, Corinth, in distant Greece. Later, the church came to appreciate Paul's statesmanship, as he bound these scattered communities into one 'body of Christ'; and his indomitable courage under many afflictions.

Paul himself marvelled at 'hard' work he had been enabled to do 'from Jerusalem round about to Illyricum', covering roughly the eastern half of the Mediterranean. Even in physical terms there is something miraculous in this achievement. Paul was early described as 'a man little of stature, thin-haired upon the head, crooked in the legs, of good state of body, with eyebrows joining and a nose somewhat crooked; full of grace, for sometimes he appeared like a man, and sometimes had the face of an angel'.

This unflattering portrait occurs in a religious romance written about the middle of the second century, but presumably it preserves some tenuous memory. At least it harmonizes with what the Corinthians said of Paul, 'his bodily presence is weak, and his speech of no account'; and with his confessed weakness on entering Galatia, and again on arriving at Corinth (Galatians 4:11, 1 Corinthians 2:3). We read elsewhere of his poor sight, needing 'large letters', and hindering recognition of the High Priest (Galatians 4:15, 6:11, Acts 23:5), and of some painful, disabling 'thorn in the flesh' which hampered him.

And yet this unprepossessing, vulnerable man proved extraordinarily resilient. His four long journeys by sea and land covered much of the known world, at a time when travel lacked comfort and security. He speaks of 'far greater labours' than some self-styled apostles endured, 'far more imprisonments, with countless beatings, often near death', five times flogged, three times beaten with rods, once stoned, three times shipwrecked, 24 hours adrift at sea, in continual danger from rivers, robbers, his own people, Gentiles, in the city, in the wilderness, at sea, and from false brethren; 'in toil and hardship, through many a sleepless night, in hunger and thirst, often without food, in cold and exposure'. Yet he can claim, in face of 'tribulation, distress, persecution, famine, nakedness, peril, sword', to be more than conqueror through Christ.

At least one young lad, timid to the point of cowardice, hearing the story of how Paul at Lystra was stoned, dragged out of the city, assumed to be dead, but the next day calmly went on to Derbe, was kindled to wonder for the very first time 'Would following Jesus do that for me, too?' But heroic courage was only one element in a personality that, despite its handicaps, evoked remarkable responses from others. One audience would pay divine honours to Paul as Hermes, messenger of the gods; responsible elders at Ephesus wept and embraced him on learning they would see him no more. Weak, aged, and ill, he remained centre of a team of young devotees. Soldiers and crew of a stricken ship listened with respect to the calm old man and accepted his advice.

Experienced Roman officials, like profligate Festus and cynical Herod, trembled and protested before him. Paul himself knew that power went out of him; he reminds Corinthians of the vital difference between instructors and fathers, and of preaching 'in demonstration of the Spirit and power'. So very often Paul's words kindled faith in others, revived drooping hopes, opened windows of vision, rebuked wrong, reawakened conscience, and fired zeal.

We speak of 'personal magnetism', 'charismatic appeal'; Paul was careful always to attribute the power that worked through him to the Christ he served, the Spirit who enabled him. For Paul was himself aware of paradox in his daily experience: as others saw a towering figure of little stature, heard an 'unimpressive' yet powerful speaker, so he was conscious of being 'famous yet unknown, dying yet alive, sorrowful yet always rejoicing, poor yet making many rich, having nothing yet possessing all things'. All Christians live within the tension between what is of themselves and what is possible by the enabling of Christ; with Paul that tension was at its sharpest and set within contradictions that challenge explanation.

An Academic Without Pride

Paul was an academic by temperament and training, with a powerful mind, considerable debating skill, and a sound knowledge of the history and religion of his people. He studied at Judaism's equivalent of a University under one of the greatest rabbis, and outstripped his fellow-students in learning and in zeal.

Some understand Acts 26:10 to imply that early in life Paul became a member of the Jewish ruling council, the Sanhedrin, though 'I cast my vote' might be merely metaphorical. But Paul's range of knowledge was wider than Jewish culture. At Athens he made effective use of pagan poetic quotations, possibly hackneyed ones; and he was familiar with the language of ancient athletics — over 50 echoes can be caught in writings attributed to him (1 Corinthians 9:24–27, Philippians 3:12–14). This knowledge could be derived from the Tarsian 'Olympic Games', though these would be forbidden to the son of strict Jewish parents.

More surprising, perhaps, are ideas like 'conscience', understood as inward awareness of the moral law, and 'self-sufficiency', meaning independence of circumstances. These, together with readiness to assess and reform social trends, self-examination, prayer, and the 'deep things of the soul' were familiar themes in Stoicism.

Much of Paul's language about divine lordship, 'union' with a divine Lord, salvation from sin and death, eternal life, the Christian 'mystery', the sacred meal of communion with God, can be paralleled in the confused teaching of the 'Mystery Cults' widespread in the Graeco-Roman world. Such echoing of language, very different from borrowing of meaning, is evidence of an alert mind determined to communicate new truth in familiar terms to the hearers.

Most surprising, though, is Paul's familiarity with the foremost theme of Greek higher education, 'rhetoric', the art of discussion, public speaking, criticism, essential to the 'democracy' of which Greece boasted. This was the 'eloquent ... wisdom of the world' which Paul expressly repudiated in preaching and writing to the Corinthians, having resolved to rest their faith upon Christ crucified, and on the demonstration of spiritual power through proclamation of the truth. Yet a careful examination of his argument in 1 Corinthians 1:17–4:21 shows Paul employing no less than 23 out of the 28 recognized devices of rhetoric — metaphor, irony, paradox, apostrophe, metonymy, questions, antithesis and the rest — over 130 times in 53 verses! Almost certainly this was a facility of which Paul himself was hardly aware, doubtless gained from long evangelizing in the educated world.

Small wonder that Paul became the highly-qualified teacher of the new faith, exploring and expounding Christian experience and working out answers to problems and misunderstandings that afflicted his mission-churches. In this way he became not only the foremost Christian theologian of the apostolic and subsequent ages, but the teaching-pastor of congregations throughout the Roman empire, and through every land in every generation since.

The paradox here lies in the sense Paul possessed of being 'indebted' — under personal obligation — not only to the wise but to the foolish, to 'barbarians', those deprived of conventional culture. 'Do not be proud,' Paul urges the Romans, 'be willing to associate with people of lowly position. Do not be conceited'. Later in the same letter we read of Paul vigorously defending the weak in judgement against the overbearing contempt of self-appointed arbiters of conduct. We still feel the strong concern and warm sympathy Paul has for the victims, even while striving to clarify their understanding.

Similarly, we marvel that a man of so great intellectual gifts could create at Corinth a congregation including 'not many wise ... the foolish in the world ... the weak, the low and despised'. And again in correspondence with them he shows his sympathy with the less gifted by acknowledging that not all possess knowledge, and some who claim it are merely 'puffed up'. The really important thing, he tells both groups, is to *love* God, and *be known by him*. So, too, he appeals with the meekness and gentleness of Christ to the 'foolish' Galatians.

This pastoral identification with the weak and under-privileged, the slow of mind and timid of faith, is as truly characteristic of Paul as are his learning and mental acumen. When the simple faith of Colossian Christians was being undermined by the intellectual pretensions of the too-clever, Paul, the academic, sternly warned against those who preyed upon others by displays of 'hollow and deceptive philosophy'. In theory, of course, the one infallible proof of a thorough education is ability to understand those less favoured. In practice, this intellectual breadth and generosity is so rare as to be a mark of exceptional grace.

A Jewish Universalist

Such wide sympathies are even more remarkable when combined with passionate religious conviction. Paul was 'a Hebrew born and bred' (NEB) inheriting all the deepest assumptions of Judaism about the living God as creator and king; about history as the arena of God's purposes; about man as made in God's image for God; about divine self-revelation through Nature, law, history and individual prophets; about the divine plan to save the world through the Jews with the help of Messiah. He inherited, too, a love of the Jewish scriptures and a clear grasp of their inmost truth.

Moreover, Paul belonged to the strictest Jewish sect, the Pharisees, devoted to everything distinctively Jewish, especially the ancient law. And Paul remained a Jew. Long after his conversion, Paul still rehearses with patriotic pride the religious 'advantages' of being a Jew (Romans 3:1-2, 9:4-5, Philippians 3:4-6).

To the end of his life the Temple, the Jewish festivals, Judaist vows of devotion, rites of purification, and the required dues and sacrifices, still constrained his conscience (Acts 18:18, 20:16, 21:26, 22:17, 24:18) as the great promises and predictions of the Old Testament still comforted his heart. It is startling to find Paul, more than 20 years a Christian, echoing the noble words of Moses in wishing that he himself might be 'accursed and cut off from Christ' if thereby his brethren Israel might be saved. Patriotic religious devotion could hardly go further.

And yet, incredibly, Paul gloried in the role of 'apostle to the Gentiles', commissioned by God 'to bear his name before the Gentiles'. It is true that birth in a pagan city, Tarsus in Cilicia, on great trade routes by sea and land, where east met west, began preparation for this dual role. So, too, did his inheritance of the freedom of Rome, his acquaintance with Greek culture, his familiarity with the scriptures in Greek translation, and with synagogues thronged with 'God-fearers' — Gentiles attracted to Jewish monotheism, worship and ethics but unwilling to become full converts.

Paul may well have heard, too, of attempts to represent Judaism persuasively to thoughtful Gentiles. To this extent, Paul's later question, 'Is God the

God of the Jews only, is he not the God of the Gentiles also?' had already faced him in pre-Christian days.

Disappointment with Judaism and the inability of law to save; Jewry's crucifying of the Christ, so betraying its privilege and destiny and deserving 'wrath, indignation, tribulation and anguish'; and awareness that legalism fostered self-righteousness and hypocrisy, may have prepared for Paul's world mission, but provide no complete explanation. Similar disillusion moved men like Ezekiel and Ezra to greater exclusiveness; it led Paul to wonder if the divine purpose might not embrace other nations beside Israel.

Pharisaism itself, as Jesus remarked, scoured sea and land to make one Gentile into a convert to Jewry. Paul's purpose, on the other hand, was to make Christian Gentiles. He argues indignantly against attempts to impose Jewish legalism, food taboos, circumcision and ideas of merit before God upon his Gentile converts. He himself, by free choice, maintained a Jewish piety; he would by no means allow Jewish religious regulations to be inflicted upon Gentile Christians as conditions of salvation.

For Paul's approach to the Gentile world was neither to confront, nor to exploit, but — most surprisingly — to appreciate the universal revelation of God to mankind. According to Luke, Paul declared that God had 'made from one every nation of men to live on all the face of the earth . . . that they should seek God, in the hope that they might feel after him and find him'. Though in past generations 'he allowed all the nations to walk in their own ways, yet he did not leave himself without witness', doing good and 'giving rains and fruitful seasons . . . food and gladness' (Acts 17:26,27, 14:16,17).

These unexpectedly 'universalist' insights are pursued in the forceful argument that 'what can be known about God is plain to all men; God has shown it to them; ever since creation his invisible nature, eternal power, and deity, have been clearly perceived in the things that are made'. Those who turned to idols are, therefore, without excuse. Moreover, 'when Gentiles, who have not the law, do by nature what the law requires . . . they show that what the law requires is written on their hearts' (Romans 1:19,20, 2:14,15).

The same broad outlook is implied in the universal offer of the gospel (Romans 10:9–13), in the view of Christ as agent of universal creation (Colossians 1:15–17), as Lord of all (Philippians 2:9–11), as comparable with Adam (not Abraham, Romans 5:12–20, 1 Corinthians 15:45–49); in his conception of God as 'Father from whom every family on earth is named' (Ephesians 3:14, 1 Corinthians 8:6), and indeed in Paul's chosen title, 'Apostle of the Gentiles' (Romans 11:13).

Hindsight may discover providential preparation for this astonishing breadth of vision, but the wonder remains that one so imbued with Jewish tradition could yet embrace men and women of all nations and cultures, and offer them on equal terms the same gospel and the fellowship of one church — as one 'people of God'! Holding that in Christ there *is* neither Jew nor Greek, but all are one, Paul was pledged to 'warn *every man* . . . teach *every man* and present *every man* mature in Christ'.

The spiritual, psychological, and racial tensions involved in such comprehensiveness are with us to this day. If many Christians overcome them, it is largely due to Paul's understanding of Jesus.

Treasure in a Clay Pot

Had Paul's contemporaries been able to foresee his historic stature they would have been still more amazed. Even a preliminary summary of his significance places him alone, as a creative, compelling personality. Paul's great truth was 'salvation by faith alone', available, therefore, to all men, freely; his great monument lay in numerous Christian communities established around the Mediterranean; his great legacy is his priceless correspondence.

Because of what Paul grasped and taught, the church passed the frontiers of Palestine and left Judaism behind. Because of what Paul did, the church survived the destruction of Jewry, and later the collapse of the Roman empire, and lived on through the dark ages. Because of what Paul experienced and movingly told, the revelation that had come to men in Christ was expounded, translated, and established as a world faith.

Nor is this assessment merely ancient eulogy or traditional reverence. In an age more inclined to denigrate great men than to appreciate them, remarkable tributes are still paid to Paul by competent judges:

- 'One of the most influential teachers of mankind'.
- 'An exceptional man, the maker of an epoch'.
- 'By far the greatest figure of his time'.
- 'The most powerful human personality in the history of the church . . . the influence of Pauline theology has permeated all subsequent theology'.
- 'While many figures of the past are unintelligible and incomprehensible, Paul is as human as if he had walked in upon us out of the street'.
- 'If the first century is the great watershed of western civilization, and religion its perennial spring, it is in the person of Paul that the Hebrew and Christian treasures of that age are mediated to ours'.
- 'History's greatest saint'.

So say the scholars. To ordinary Christians, Paul is usually 'the great apostle', his writings 'scripture', and his life-work ascribed directly to his Lord. There could be no higher assessment. But is this saying too much? A few have deliberately discarded the gospels and held Paul the real founder of Christianity. More have preferred to quote Paul's words, rather than those of

Jesus, as 'more relevant' to the age between the advents. But no man in history would have repudiated this extravagant idea more vehemently than Paul himself. Indeed, he does so, in no uncertain fashion! 'Was Paul crucified for you? or were you baptised in the name of Paul?' 'Other foundation can no man lay than that is laid, which is Christ Jesus.' 'Even if we, or an angel from heaven, should preach to you a gospel contrary to that which we preached to you, let him be accursed!' 'I determined to know nothing among you save Christ, and him crucified.' Paul's own answer to the question 'What is Paul?' was 'A servant...'

A man may be a living miracle (every Christian is, to some extent) without becoming infallible. Paul has not escaped criticism. Some former complaints against him have evaporated with better understanding. 'He loved long, complicated sentences!' — modern translations render what was acceptable and clear in Greek into the peculiarities of English with its love of full-stops.

'Paul delighted in argumentation!' — his letters were usually evoked by urgent problems, difficulties and confusions in his infant churches, issues that had to be carefully argued out; only in *Romans*, and a few speeches in *Acts*, do we possess anything of his quiet, constructive, free thought.

'Paul was only a theologian!' — no one who knows his adventurous life-story, and his daily involvement in the life of the churches, could possibly think of Paul as a *mere* academic, with his head in the clouds.

Yet Paul certainly did not consider himself infallible, or invulnerable. He confesses that he regretted writing one letter. He concedes, repeatedly, that he is writing, or boasting 'like a fool'. In one unguarded quotation he urges the Christian to feed his enemy 'for by so doing you will heap living coals upon his head'! He made plans — to visit Corinth, to evangelize Spain — that were never fulfilled. He often confesses that he does not know what God plans for him, but must wait to see 'how things will go' (Philippians 1:22, 2:23). He sometimes needed to explain more carefully counsel he had given that was ambiguous (as to Corinth), or less than satisfactory (as to Thessalonica). A few of Paul's interpretations of scripture reflect more rabbinic 'spiritualizing' than historical accuracy (see Galatians 4:21–31, 1 Corinthians 10:1–4, Romans 9–11), though each argument would be compelling for the readers addressed.

Some of Paul's actions, too, though they can be honestly defended, do require defence — his brusque treatment of Mark, his reaction to Elymas (though he *may* have remembered that blindness led his own soul to see Christ clearly!), his 'reviling' of the High Priest, his deliberate provoking of discord between parties in the Sanhedrin, which settled nothing.

Paul did occasionally change his opinion about individuals (2 Corinthians 2:5–8, Colossians 4:10, see 2 Timothy 4:10), which might look like faulty judgement. And one great uncertainty, to be considered in its proper place, raises the question whether at the end Paul's character lost something of its earlier grace and patience.

As for vulnerability, the apostle does not pretend to be immune to the temptations 'common to man'. It is not difficult to perceive behind the memories unfolded in Romans 7 the story of a soul passing from innocence through 'coveting', and forbidding, to the discovery of inner sinfulness and a 'captivity' in which phrases like 'I am carnal, sold under sin', 'nothing good dwells within me, that is, in my flesh', 'another law in my members at war with the law of my mind . . . the law of sin which dwells in my members' clearly suggest the familiar struggles of adolescence.

Slight echoes, here, of the Eden story tend to confirm this meaning; it was an axiom of Pharisaic psychology that each man is the 'Adam' of his own soul. Some of Paul's words about marriage as the cure for inordinate passion, and his testimony, 'I do not run aimlessly . . . I pommel my body and subdue it, lest . . . I myself should be disqualified', likewise acknowledge a sense of the dangers of the 'mind set on the flesh'.

Of another kind is the fear of being disappointed in people (2 Corinthians 12:20 — at least five times); and of becoming spiritually conceited through the revelations granted to him, for so he understood his 'thorn in the flesh'. The fear of boasting is mentioned over 50 times: doubtless this is where the Christian shoe most sharply pinched the ex-Pharisee's foot! The boasting of the Jew in his election, his merits, his self-righteousness, is totally excluded by a gospel of salvation by faith alone, but old habits of self-congratulation die hard. Paul recognized his own weaknesses.

A more surprising self-revelation is Paul's vulnerability to criticism. He could be stung by jibes, deeply hurt by accusations, sorely upset by disrupted relations with his converts, as at Corinth. Especially painful was the repeated accusation that he was no true apostle, having never been in the company of Jesus, and so lacking the authority of the original Twelve. That suggestion undermined the confidence of his converts, and, to judge from his replies, touched a sore spot of insecurity within the apostle, too.

Some of the Corinthians, offended that he had not visited them as early as they expected, accused him of vacillation, and he devotes some vigorous verses to his retort. Some at Galatia were challenging his authority to define the terms of salvation, and he gives nearly 40 careful verses to this theme, before challenging his rivals' motives. In gentler tones he deals with a suggestion that he had neglected the church at Rome.

It is, however, in 2 Corinthians 10–13 that we learn how deeply Paul could be wounded. Harsh words are sharply remembered, vehemently rejected — charges that he is humble when present, bold only at a distance; that he writes weightily but his speech is of no account; that there is no proof that Christ speaks through him. Some said he was too proud to accept support, that he was crafty and got the better of them by guile. The whole passage vibrates with hurt feeling, mingling riposte, challenge, and tender sadness.

Yet, perhaps, the effect of such attitudes upon the generous out-reaching spirit of Paul is most vividly seen in his unexpected confession that when he reached Troas, and opportunity was given to preach Christ, his mind could not rest for lack of news from troubled Corinth. The zealous, indomitable evangelist, whom no threats, persecution or peril could ever deter, was silenced by anxiety and regret.

Obviously, the great apostle was very human. Admiration, hero-worship, reverence, must not become idolatry. Paul's total dedication to Christ, his exceptional gifts and energy, afford him a place in Christian history shared by very few. But Paul knew himself a sinner saved and sustained only by the grace of God in Christ. He never pretended otherwise to himself, nor hesitated to admit it to others.

This is, of course, the sharpest of the Pauline paradoxes: that one so hampered and fallible could achieve so much, bless so many, and initiate so limitless and timeless a ministry of grace.

'We have this treasure in earthen vessels,' Paul explains, 'to show that the transcendent power belongs to God and not to us ... I will all the more gladly boast of my weaknesses, that the power of Christ may rest upon me. For the sake of Christ, then, I am content with weaknesses, insults, hardships, persecutions, calamities; *for when I am weak, then am I strong.*'

This view of man, as a vehicle of powers greater than his own, good or evil as he shall choose, runs throughout the Bible, but is nowhere better illustrated than in Paul. Ephesus provides but one, wholly typical, example. Paul says that there he fought with beasts, was utterly unbearably crushed, despaired of life. Luke says Ephesus saw his greatest triumph, with the idol-makers' protest quenched by the town-clerk, a fortune in magic-books burned in the market place, a centre of evangelism established that became mother-church of at least seven others.

Therein lies Paul's own secret of his astonishing story. It was all miracle: 'Not I, but the Lord ... Not I, but the grace of God which is with me ... It is no longer I who live, but Christ who lives in me.'

Suggestions for Group Discussion

(Groups, or leaders, should choose which of the offered questions they will consider, or raise their own.)

1 Do you agree that 'every Christian is a living miracle to some extent'? — to what extent?

2 Evidence is offered in this chapter that Paul was open to temptation, sensitive to criticism (see 'Treasure in a Clay Pot'). Reconsidering this evidence in detail, does it diminish or enhance Paul's authority as an apostle?

3 Was Paul's effectiveness as apostle, evangelist, pastor, due to divine preparation of his personal gifts, background, Jewish training, inherited Roman freedom, or was it due to an endowment of the Spirit which could have come upon any man, however ignorant and ill-equipped?

4 Luke wrote more of the New Testament than Paul did. Would the church have been wiser to give Luke a greater place in its thinking than it has always given to Paul?

CHAPTER 2

'A Skilled Master-Builder'

Preparatory Reading: 1 Corinthians 3:10–15, Romans 2:28,29, 13:1–7, Acts 15:1–21, Galatians 2:11–16, 3:28–29

In speaking of himself as 'a skilled master-builder', Paul is not claiming cleverness, or superior wisdom, but the practical shrewdness that comes from experience. 'Building' is not his only metaphor for the ministry he pursued: he was a *sower* of seed in the field of society, a *soldier* in a militant movement, a *steward* and guardian of the riches of the gospel, an *ambassador* negotiating reconciliation, a *father* of new converts, even a *nursemaid* caring for children (1 Thessalonians 2:7). But *builder* is his favourite analogy, used nearly 30 times, including exhortations to be 'built up', to 'edify one another', to be 'built together'.

In 1 Corinthians 3:10–15 the metaphor expresses clearly Paul's main conception of his mission, the establishment of churches, and suggests several manifestations of his shrewdness in the task. In the Roman world, it mattered greatly upon what 'foundation' Christian life was built, on philosophic theorizing about life, upon infectious emotional thrills, upon propagandists' eloquence, mysterious rites, occult superstitions.

When Paul reminded the Corinthians that he had laid the foundation on which rested their faith in the power of God as manifested in Christ crucified, he was recalling them to the basis of all Christian experience, what God had shown and done in the person, life, death and resurrection of Christ the Lord.

Christ the Foundation

'No other foundation can anyone lay than that which is laid, which is Jesus Christ'. Paul's meaning is best illustrated by careful examination of his evangelistic preaching. When the evidence is meticulously assembled one detail is immediately obvious: *every time* Paul's preaching is described, its central content is — Christ. Seven times the emphasis falls upon Jesus risen from the dead, and Festus, like the Athenians, took this to be Paul's main theme. Eleven times Jesus is described as Christ, the Son, the Lord of all. At Athens and Miletus, to Agrippa and Felix, Paul preached Jesus as judge.

In perfect truth the apostle could claim 'We preach not ourselves, but

Christ Jesus the Lord . . . Christ the power of God and the wisdom of God', the only enduring foundation of any Christian life and any Christian church. The shrewd builder knew his responsibility.

But with equal shrewdness and skill Paul strove to present his one message in ways appropriate to differing audiences. Wherever possible the synagogue was his springboard, and there he argued from Israel's history and law like any visiting rabbi.

At Philippi, lacking a synagogue, Paul joined a small local prayer-group at the riverside. At Lystra he proceeded like any market place evangelist; at Athens like any peripatetic Stoic debater; at Ephesus he hired a public lecture hall and 'entertained' the curious with religious discussion. At Paphos, Paul seems to have approached the resident official in private; in Rome he received a large deputation of enquirers for a day's debate about Christ's claim. The message was always the same, its presentation shaped by local circumstances, an essential tactic of evangelism.

But such 'localizing' of the gospel went further. In Jerusalem, Paul joined other Christians at the Temple; elsewhere he joined the worship at a synagogue. At Syrian Antioch, Christians met separately for prophesying, teaching, and prayer; at Corinth a formless spontaneity of worship appears to have been practised.

The same variety marks church order. At Jerusalem, a band of apostles under James' presidency was in charge; at Ephesus and elsewhere, a group of senior Christians (elders) exercised oversight; at Philippi we read later of 'bishops' (overseers) and deacons. Later still apostolic appointees select elders and amend what is defective. At Corinth, the whole membership assembled to make decisions (see 1 Corinthians 5:4–5).

It takes a far-seeing mind to concentrate upon what is essential — the revelation of God in Christ — and let its cultural expression in presentation, worship, government, vary with local tradition. The wise master-builder sets the foundation deep, but uses local stone and style, harmonizing his architecture with the local community as a 'native' creation.

Sharing the Building

The other implication which Paul draws from his metaphor in 1 Corinthians is that others may — indeed must — extend and consolidate what the founder begins. There is risk here, for others may build of wood, wattle, thatch, or of gold, silver, precious stones. Christ's Day will disclose what has been faithfully built and will survive. But God's work is no individual worker's preserve, or private hobby.

Strange as it may seem, Paul was essentially a team-man. Someone has counted 67 named colleagues and associates of Paul; someone else makes it

83! Many are so familiar to us — Timothy, Silas, Tychicus, Barnabas, Titus, Luke, Aristarchus, Epaphras, Philemon, Priscilla, Aquila — that it is obvious Paul's greatness overshadowed none of them. There was no attempt to 'lord it over' any one else's service (see 2 Corinthians 1:24); when Apollos did not feel it right to do what Paul urged, the decision must be his own (1 Corinthians 16:12). Moreover, Paul fully appreciated, and often praised, the many kinds of service, different from his own, which other Christians rendered (1 Corinthians 12:4,11, 28–30).

Paul's was a much more affectionate and social nature than is commonly supposed. One colleague is a 'true yokefellow', another 'my brother and fellow worker and fellow soldier', another 'a beloved brother and faithful minister and fellow servant', and yet another 'our beloved fellow servant'. Luke is 'the beloved physician'. When some at Corinth tried to make Apollos Paul's rival, Paul insisted upon treating him as an equal and a friend.

Significantly, Paul invented a number of these 'fellow-' words, using 34 in all, to convey his deep sense of shared experience, shared labour, shared suffering. They include fellow-partakers, fellow-comforters, fellow-prisoners, fellow-imitators, fellow-refreshed, fellow-growing, even fellows in fellowship. It is not graciousness alone which thus emphasizes working together with others in the service of Christ, but spiritual wisdom.

With all this, Paul contrived to combine brotherliness with the authority inherent, not in any personal qualities, or merely in the office he held, but in the truth he taught, the Lord he represented. He could admonish severely: 'What do you wish, shall I come to you with a rod? ... I am prepared to court-martial everyone who is insubordinate (Moffatt) ... If I boast a little too much of our authority which the Lord gave for building you up ... I shall be justified ... I warned those who sinned ... if I come again I will not spare ... Such persons we command in the Lord'. Ministry without authority is pathetic. But so is authority without humility. Paul could still insist that he was only 'a servant through whom you believed', and decline to visit the Corinthians until assured of their welcome.

A Wide Foundation

A third feature of the foundation Paul laid, though not mentioned in *Corinthians*, is its breadth. Rome had unified almost the known world under the Caesars: Paul aimed at a kingdom of Christ that had the same scope as the empire. *Acts* recounts his covering of the eastern Mediterranean except for north Africa, and it is instructive to follow the story with a map of Roman communications. Two facts become clear: Paul made good use of the main Roman road system and sea routes; and he concentrated mainly upon great centres of population and power.

Paul began his mission on Cyprus, home of his colleague and senior, Barnabas, but soon he was venturing on to the mainland of Asia Minor, past Perga to the great road junction of Pisidian Antioch, a Roman colony. Iconium, Lystra, Derbe are the next three towns on the great road running eastward through Cilicia to Syria. Ephesus was a great centre of culture and religion, a seaport, and focus of the wide hinterland of Roman Asia, with numerous towns that became famous in Christian history — Smyrna, Laodicea, Hierapolis, Colossae among them. Troas was another seaport on a great road through Asia Minor, the embarkation point for Europe.

Philippi, a proud Roman colony, dominated eastern Macedonia, and was the entry-point by land for Europe. Thessalonica, on the famous Via Egnatia, the overland route to Italy, was the chief town in western Macedonia; Paul speaks of touching even Illyricum, facing the Adriatic sea, possibly at this time. For centuries Athens had been the intellectual capital of the world, and remained the centre of the Greek world. Corinth was the greatest city of Greece, on the main sea route through the Mediterranean, another meeting-place of east and west, crowded with travellers and sailors from every known country. *At all these places Paul established centres of evangelism and outreach.*

This was magnificent missionary planning. Paul held his special commission to be pioneering: 'my ambition, to preach the gospel not where Christ has already been named'. Pioneering involved self-support by daily work, in Paul's case as a 'tentmaker' (either in woven goats-hair or in leather), until a local Christian community could release him for full-time evangelism. The extra labour was considerable, but the independence, and freedom from any charge of preaching for gain, made it worth while.

In addition, Paul's churches were taught to be self-propagating. Any one of these main areas he visited could have absorbed Paul's energies for life, had he travelled the valleys, minor roads, daughter towns and villages. But local Christians could do that, multiplying the pioneer's impact many times.

At the same time, Paul guarded against the one danger inherent in this strategy, that of creating isolated communities unrelated to each other, partly by his doctrine of one 'body of Christ'. In addition, his repeated visits to established churches made him the personal link between them, supplemented by his team of messengers, like Timothy, Titus, Tychicus, and others.

Further, he maintained a pastoral correspondence which counselled and strengthened the churches while also linking them together by news, shared problems, and mutual prayer. And he encouraged each church to show hospitality towards Christians travelling on business or imperial journeys.

The lasting result of this incomparable missionary wisdom is clear. When the original home of Christianity was destroyed in AD 70, and the mother-church at Jerusalem scattered beyond Judea, the foundations of the new faith had been so broadly laid — even geographically — that the church proved indestructible.

Guarding the Building

Paul's skill as a master-builder is revealed no less in his clear perception of the dangers amidst which his converts must live, and the steps he took to arm the churches to face them. Here the realism of Paul's shrewdness is clearly illustrated. His unwavering faith in divine help, his spiritual zeal and vision, his measureless courage, are all tempered by a down-to-earth common sense that makes a formidable combination. There were three specific dangers to guard against.

Paul's churches had to live and work under the most powerful military dictatorship in history. Paul valued those features of Roman rule which assisted his work — universal 'peace', ease of communications, social order, impartial justice — and submitted readily to Rome's legal forms at Philippi, Corinth, Ephesus, Jerusalem and Caesarea. But the legal status of Christianity remained ambiguous. After long struggles, Judaism was an officially protected religion, and Christianity began as a sect within Judaism (Acts 24:5,14, 28: 22), sharing this protection. Orthodox Jews resented this, accusing Christians (and the renegade ex-Pharisee Paul, especially) of usurping Jewish privileges. In city after city, there was trouble in the synagogues over Paul's message, and Jewish mobs beset Paul, accusing him before the courts (as at Thessalonica, Corinth) in order to dissociate themselves in Roman eyes from Christian 'subversion'.

One safeguard against trouble with the State was to teach converts the obligations of good citizenship. The Christian reaction to persecution was not defiance, threats, or contempt, but a standard of social responsibility, and support for all that is good in the State, that shall disarm opposition. Christians should aspire to live quietly, mind their own affairs, work well with their hands, so as to command the respect of outsiders, above reproach (1 Thessalonians 2:10, 3:13, 4:11, 5:23).

With every Jew, Paul traced 'the governing authorities' back to God's institution of social order; to resist just laws was to resist the divine appointment, and so incur God's judgement, of which human judges and magistrates were God's agents. Conscience, therefore, as well as fear, counselled submission, the payment of taxes, respect, and honour (Romans 13:1–7). (According to 1 Timothy 2:1–3, Paul also exhorted congregations to pray, and to give thanks for kings and all in high positions in the State, that Christians might enjoy a peaceable life.)

As the church became increasingly Gentile, and the breach with Judaism widened, the shelter of a 'legal religion' became less secure. Rome suspected all private societies and groupings of subversive intentions (Acts 17:6,7), while disaffected individuals (as at Philippi), or craftsmen's guilds (as at Ephesus), or Jewish congregations (as at Corinth) found other reasons for opposing the new faith.

At Philippi, unjustly beaten and imprisoned, Paul would not leave the city until the full apology of the magistrates threw protection round the little Christian 'cell' he was leaving behind. At Corinth, the famous proconsul Gallio, at Ephesus the town clerk, defended Paul. At Jerusalem the military tribune delivered him from conspiracy. At Caesarea, first the governor Felix declined to pass verdict, then the governor Festus agreed with Herod Agrippa, Rome's adviser on Jewish affairs, that Paul should be set free.

But by that time Paul had sought to lift the whole issue out of the hands of Jewish accusers and local magistrates, because the future of Christianity in the empire was at stake. He sought universal legal recognition of the faith, and, at great risk, focused the issue in his own case by appealing to Caesar's judgement. Such an appeal by a free Roman citizen could not be denied, and Paul was sent to Rome for trial. On the journey, the centurion in charge of prisoners learned to trust Paul and treated him with respect, but in Rome itself things went badly wrong. The details are obscure, but it is clear that Rome's attitude towards the new religion had hardened into suspicion, Christians had been made scapegoats for every oppression, misfortune, and disaster, and Paul died at the hands of a half-mad emperor.

Nevertheless Paul's strategy reflected the highest Christian statesmanship. His training of Christians in citizenship, and his repeated warnings to converts that 'through many tribulations we must enter the kingdom of God', prepared them for trouble without encouraging any one to seek martyrdom. But if the tension between loyalty to Christ the Lord and loyalty to the civic authorities became stretched to breaking point, because the State sought obedience beyond its proper jurisdiction, then the Christian must be faithful unto death.

Paul's intention in appealing to Caesar was excellent, its motive far-seeing, while behind it lay the realization that the church must come to terms with the world as it is. Paul would co-operate with just authority in the State to the limit of his conscience; pressed beyond that, he would — and did — die.

A Racial Dilemma

The same practical wisdom is evident in Paul's awareness of the second danger facing his infant churches, that of being submerged within Judaism, as another sect like the Pharisees, Essenes, Sadducees; or becoming for all time divided into Jewish versus Gentile 'denominations'. For the same strong tensions which Paul, as the intensely Jewish apostle of the Gentiles, had faced within himself and so remarkably overcame by the greatness of his mind and heart, faced him again in the developing church. It is difficult for us to feel now the overwhelming importance of this problem; the immediate danger passed with time, but the issues involved are perennial.

Born out of Judaism and the Jewish hope of Messiah, appealing to the Jewish scriptures and enjoying the legal protection Judaism had won, Christianity could so easily have remained Jewish, forever bound in the narrow legalism, nationalism, and ritualism, which kept Jewry closed to the wider world. Any Gentiles attracted by the gospel would then need to become Jews before accepting Christ. Their salvation would rest on obedience to Jewish law, tradition, and piety, illumined by the teaching of Jesus.

Against this possibility, in theory, Paul affirmed strongly (as his letters show) his gospel of salvation by faith in Christ *alone*, which plainly was available to all races equally. To possess Abraham's faith was to *be* a true Jew, one of God's elect, for in Christ there is no Jewish-Gentile distinction. In practice, Paul resisted equally strongly any imposition upon his Gentile converts of Jewish food taboos, circumcision, sabbaths, festivals. They remained *Gentiles*, though Christian Gentiles. By Paul's penetrating understanding and firm leadership, the danger of submergence within Judaism was resolutely and finally removed.

But the opposite danger loomed the more threateningly, that the church would then divide into distinct Jewish and Gentile sections, alienated, and perhaps irreconcilable. The gulf which for centuries, and in every respect, had separated Jew and Gentile could so easily be reproduced within the church.

We see the gulf beginning to appear at the objection of Christian Jews to the conversion of Cornelius; at the refusal of Peter and others to eat with Gentile Christians at Syrian Antioch; and in the caution with which even Paul was received by the mother-church at Jerusalem. 'You see, brother, how many thousands there are among the Jews of those who have believed; they are all zealous for the law, and they have been told about you that you teach all the Jews who are among the Gentiles to forsake Moses, telling them not to circumcise their children or observe the customs. What then is to be done? They will certainly hear that you have come.' So said James, and the Jerusalem elders (Acts 21:20–22). All the suspicion and fear of Christian Jewry is in their words.

Once again the wisdom of the skilled master-builder was equal to the need, as he took deliberate steps to avert any such break. Early in his Christian life he visited the leaders of the Jewish church to 'lay before them the gospel' which he preached, and to receive 'the right hand of fellowship' as one commissioned to the Gentiles even as Peter was to the Jews. When Timothy, of mixed parentage, joined his team, he had him circumcised 'because of the Jews that were in those places'. So narrow, sometimes, is the line between conciliation and compromise!

On that last visit to Jerusalem, Paul accepted James' advice, to allay Jewish suspicions, by showing himself for his own part still living 'in observance of the law'. In *Romans*, he reminds Gentile Christians that Israel was privileged, and had been blessed, and will yet be blessed. The Gentiles must not boast, but remember what they owe to Israel — the root and stem which supports their branches. In *Ephesians*, Paul lists the privileges of Israel into which Gentiles have been brought by the gospel, ending in a warning that the building of God must be firmly 'bonded together' (NEB).

And at the close of his mission in the east, Paul's last great act was to organize among his largely Gentile churches massive relief for Christians in Palestine in material need. It was a magnanimous gesture of unity in Christ and of Gentile gratitude to Jewish Christianity. The operation took two or three years, and delegates from each contributing church helped him carry it to Jerusalem, 'aiming at what is honourable . . . in the sight of men', but also cementing unity by personal contact (Acts 20:3–5).

That Paul considered this mission of reconciliation as inspired by God is clear from his request for prayer that it might be accepted (Romans 15:30–31), and his insistence upon carrying it out in the face of the most solemn warnings (Acts 21:10–14). Paul could hardly have done more to defend Gentile equality with Jews in the body of Christ, and yet preserve the unity of both in the new Israel of God.

Moral Armour

And Paul showed the same skill and foresight in anticipating the third danger to his churches, the insidious pressures of a largely decadent society. In some respects this was a new problem, for in general in the ancient world religion was not morally demanding, or uplifting. Tales told of the gods and goddesses, and some forms of pagan 'worship', including drunkenness and prostitution, actually encouraged vice. Tender Greek and Roman consciences turned for support to philosophy rather than to religion. Christianity, on the other hand, inherited beside the high ethical monotheism of Israel, and the social teaching of the great prophets, the inspiring ideal of Jesus.

Paul's picture of the age was critical, even pessimistic, showing in darkest colours the sensuality, violence, divisiveness, and vice, that corrupted contemporary society (Romans 1:26–32, 2 Thessalonians 2:3–12). To be a

Christian in such a hostile climate called for considerable moral heroism, and wisdom.

Despite his passion for evangelism, Paul never minimized the negative aspects of the Christian message. A clean break must be made with past evil; Christians 'died with Christ' to self, to sin, and to the allurements of the sinful world. There was need, for beginners at any rate, to 'come out from among' former sinful companionships, to no longer touch, or talk about, unclean things. The world that could crucify Jesus was no spiritual home for hearts that love him; to 'mind earthly things' spelled spiritual death.

Without such warning the new convert would remain dangerously vulnerable. Three times Paul urges preparation in militarist terms: 'put on the armour of light' (live openly in God's daylight, not in concealment); 'put on the breastplate of faith and love, and for helmet the hope of salvation'; and again 'put on the whole armour of God', each item of which has *moral* quality: truth, righteousness, peaceableness, faith, experience of salvation, the sword of the Spirit, all to be deployed with prayer and spiritual alertness. The Christian in a permissive society has a fight on his hands.

For the Roman church Paul summarized Christian moral imperatives in the love of neighbour which cannot commit adultery, kill, steal, covet, or do any wrong. Christians must renounce all that needed darkness to conceal it — revelling, drunkenness, debauchery, licentiousness, quarrelling, jealousy.

To the Thessalonians, Paul's emphasis fell upon faithfulness and purity in sexual matters, honest work to maintain independence. Elsewhere the duties of stable and affectionate home life, kindness, almsgiving, care towards children, with strict avoidance of dishonesty, slander, filthy talk, untruthfulness, incest, and all uncleanness, recur constantly in Paul's pastoral counsel.

The form of such moral armament against evil proves to be closely similar in writings of Paul, Peter, James, the letter to the Hebrews, and (without its echoes of Jesus) the synagogue's own moral education of young Jews. This suggests that such passages are meant to remind hearers of careful training already received at conversion (probably referred to in Romans 6:17, 2 Thessalonians 2:15, 1 Corinthians 11:2).

The motives urged for high moral endeavour sprang mainly from the holiness of God, which governs all religious experience; admiration and love towards Christ; and emphasis upon the indwelling of the *holy* Spirit, contrasted with the ubiquitous evil spirits.

Reinforcing such incentives was the solemn warning, 'Neither the immoral, nor idolaters, nor adulterers, nor homosexuals, nor thieves, nor the greedy, nor drunkards, nor revilers, nor robbers will inherit the kingdom of God'.

Qualities required for moral progress included wisdom in discerning what is good (frequently mentioned); a healthy self-discipline in pursuing it, which is the essence of Paul's spiritual 'athleticism' (1 Corinthians 9:24–27); and simple obedience to the word and example of Christ, reflected in senior Christians (1 Corinthians 4:16,17, Philippians 3:17).

Thus, there is about Paul's skill as a master-builder much that surely characterized the erection of some great cathedral, deeply-laid foundations, strategic planning, united efforts of varied craftsmen, wide distribution of weight, inbuilt stability against external storm, firm bonding against internal subsidence, and effective protection from the elements.

Long, changeful history has shown that the great apostle built more wisely than perhaps he himself realized.

Suggestions for Group Discussion

1 The discussion of 'Christ the Foundation' implies a clear distinction between what is central to the Christian message and the varied forms which the message, the church, worship, may take in different cultures, different generations. How does this distinction affect church life and work in these changing days — (a) at home (b) abroad?

2 What qualities make a good leader, or a good team-man/woman, in Christian work? Can they be combined in one person?

3 The section 'Guarding the Building' outlines Paul's strategy for Christians living in a hostile state: would this suffice today, under atheism or apartheid?

4 Should the church today emphasize the *negative* demands of the gospel, in protest, and protection of the weak, in a decaying society?

CHAPTER 3

A Complex Character

Preparatory Reading: Philemon, Acts 15:36–41, 1 Corinthians 5:1–8, 2 Corinthians 13:1–10, Romans 14

Some Christians do not find Paul likeable. And many who admit his considerable gifts, experience, and character, admire without being attracted. Most Christians probably hold him in such reverence that they do not even consider such a question. That is a pity, for Paul often opens his heart to us and it is churlish to ignore his appeals for understanding.

Nowhere is Paul's inner character more clearly, or more surprisingly, revealed than in his brief private note to Philemon. Admittedly, this letter is exceptional; it is the only correspondence which was not evoked by some urgent danger, serious problem, or unsought contention, apart possibly from Ephesians. Consequently, Paul can write to Philemon as a personal friend, more freely than usual, unguardedly, and with evident enjoyment.

From hints scattered through 25 verses we gather that this friend, Philemon, and his wife and son (probably), hosts to a church at or near Colossae (Colossians 4:9), have suffered the loss of a young slave, Onesimus, who has stolen from his master and fled for his life, probably to Ephesus, just possibly to Rome. Further ill-doing has brought Onesimus to prison, where he meets Paul, who leads him to Christ. The question then arises, what is to be done with him? To the apostle he has become beloved, useful, almost a son, but he belongs to Philemon, a friend and fellow-Christian. Besides, conversion is no just escape from due punishment.

For friendship's and the young man's sake, Paul sends Onesimus back to Philemon, but with such a note of explanation and entreaty as must ensure a welcome, forgiveness, and acceptance as a Christian brother, and a friend of beloved Paul! The total situation is intriguing: youth, making a bid for freedom from one kind of slavery, finds itself imprisoned; there youth meets age, also imprisoned, because voluntarily enslaved to Christ; through that encounter, youth too becomes voluntarily enslaved, and finds a total freedom beyond anything dreamed of!

Apart from the high principle embodied here, that true repentance *always* includes restoration wherever possible, we are surely compelled to warm to the old apostle, seen befriending a young man in trouble, and pledging his own good name and friendship, his own welcome in Philemon's home, to gain his forgiveness. Long before, Barnabas had done much the same for Paul. And the appeal itself is so beautifully, humorously, movingly penned.

In choice words, Paul recalls hearing of Philemon's care for the congregation meeting in his home, and says that such news enriches his prayers and comforts his heart. On that same care for Christians, Paul bases his request that Philemon will now do what Paul asks — he could command it, as an apostle and a friend, as the one to whom Philemon owes his knowledge of Christ, but he prefers to appeal, as an old man (or, possibly, 'as Christ's envoy'), as a partner with Philemon in the gospel, and 'for love's sake'. The request is 'for my child Onesimus', 'reborn in my imprisonment', 'my very heart', and 'a beloved brother'. Paul says he might have retained him, leaving Philemon no choice but to agree; but he preferred that Philemon should voluntarily consent to whatever was done, in the freedom of friendship.

Interwoven with this 'heart's argument', is a threefold pun on the name Onesimus, 'useful, beneficial, profitable'. Onesimus has indeed formerly belied his name; now he has become 'useful' again, but to Paul, and Paul wants an *'onaimen'* — 'a useful benefit' — from Philemon in exchange for Onesimus.

Added to the appeal is a careful suggestion that good can be wrought out of the unhappy story: 'perhaps he was parted from you as slave for a while that you might have him back a brother beloved in Christ, and for ever'. Then, again playfully, a formal, businesslike IOU: 'If he has wronged you, owes you anything, I will repay it; I write this in my own handwriting, I will repay it' — and then the very gentle reminder that Philemon owes Paul his very soul!

An expression of utter confidence that Philemon will do more than he is asked, and the promise of an early visit, end this charming glimpse into early Christian relationships, and give a gracious insight into 'the real Paul'. This is a different Paul from the far-seeing church builder, soldier of Christ, stormy propagandist, leader of men. At the least, we see that Paul shows both a public and a private face, not inconsistent, but certainly varying, powerful to the world, playful to his friends.

If we venture then to ask, probingly, what sort of man he was, we must concede at the outset that so profound and formidable a personality could hardly bear a simple, transparent character. The paradoxes, the superficial contradictions, observable in the circumstances and events of his public life, are reflected in the man behind the image. Nothing about him is single, uncomplicated, obvious.

A Many-sided Man

Like all strong personalities, Paul showed the defects of his qualities. His brusque treatment of Mark showed an indomitable man's impatience with an unreliable colleague, though Paul handsomely forgave Mark later (Acts 15:36–40, Colossians 4:10).

In sharp contrast was Paul's later affection for and defence of another young helper, Timothy, though he was timid, ailing, often in need of encouragement. In challenge and rebuke Paul could be formidable, yet with the struggling he could be infinitely patient. 'Who is weak and I am not weak? Who is made to fall and I am not indignant?' (2 Corinthians 11:29; see Galatians 4:19–20).

With all his high demands, Paul asked no more commitment than he himself gave; and the same mind and heart penned repeated appeals for patience, kindness, goodness, gentleness, understanding, encouragement — appeals which would have been instantly self-defeating had his own character belied them.

When the sternness shown to Corinth had done its work, the 'true Paul' wrote, 'For such an one this punishment is enough, so you should rather forgive and comfort him, or he may be overwhelmed with excessive sorrow. So I beg you to reaffirm your love for him. Any one whom you forgive ... I also forgive ...' And, however loud the Pauline thunder when storm-clouds gathered, the same mind produced the imperishable hymn to love, its importance, its nature, and its value, that is 1 Corinthians 13.

The intricate discussion in *Romans* of minor moral obligations concerning meats, drinks, holy days, which divided the Christians at Rome into the 'tough-minded', or 'strong', and the 'tender-minded', or 'weak', reveals far more than the patience of an intellectual with the weak in judgement. Here is a complex mind, an even more complex heart! So carefully balanced are Paul's arguments, and so skilfully interwoven, that some interpreters have placed Paul among the 'weak', arguing for tender scruples against the negligent 'strong'.

In truth, Paul argues for the 'strong' position, but all his sympathies and defence rally to the 'weak', who are being bullied. He places upon the 'strong' the extra obligation to bear with the 'weak', in no way to judge them, even to surrender something of their own liberty of action if the 'weak' are thereby endangered, because love is more important than freedom. And he roundly asserts that while every man shall 'to his own master stand or fall', God shall assuredly make the 'weak' to stand, however the 'strong' may despise him. It is easy to dismiss the discussion as illogical, 'having it both ways': that is untrue, for Paul makes his position perfectly clear. But faced with sensitive souls in trouble, he will not 'break a bruised reed or quench a smouldering wick' for the sake of a debater's applause. That is the complicated kind of man he was!

Humility, surely, is a simple, easily understood virtue. We all know how to define it, until we try. Paul was certainly 'humble', as his oft-repeated fear of boasting, his relationship to so many colleagues, his constant requests for prayer, his admission of the need for chastening to keep him from too great elevation, all clearly prove. 'I am the least of the apostles, unfit to be called an apostle, because I persecuted the church of God ... I am the very least of all the saints' are admissions it would be futile for any man to make who aspires to leadership and significance in others' lives, unless they were manifestly sincere, and sustained.

But Paul's is not the quality that often passes for humility, a self-deprecating refusal to serve, to accept responsibility, to offer leadership or exercise authority, 'lest we fail'. That is usually inverted pride, fearful of criticism. Paul's humility was, in part, a deep sense of privilege at being allowed to serve. It was an abiding awareness of being in debt, of having gifts, opportunities, and help, that never could be deserved. Most of all it was the realization that he owed everything good in his life to the grace of God. Such humility may be more difficult to understand, but it is far more useful, more stimulating, more sustaining under disappointment, than pretended self-depreciation.

Again, for all his ready co-operation with others, and appreciation of their fellowship, Paul retained an inward independence that is sometimes disconcerting. He rounds upon his critics at Corinth, for example, with the words, 'With me it is a very small thing that I should be judged by you, or by any human court', though the snub is softened somewhat by the admission, 'I do not even judge myself... it is the Lord who judges me'.

But the most dramatic example of such independence occurred at Caesarea, where a prophet, speaking in the name of the Holy Spirit, warned Paul of danger in going to Jerusalem, and his whole company, with the local Christians, begged him not to go. Paul replied, 'What are you doing, weeping and breaking my heart? For I am ready not only to be imprisoned but even to die at Jerusalem for the name of the Lord Jesus' — and moved forward. His plans had long been carefully made, and no persuasion of others, unaware of the importance of that contribution to the saints at Jerusalem, could move him to fear.

Another surprising retort is made to those at Galatia who challenged Paul's apostleship. 'I would have you know that the gospel which I preached is not man's gospel. For I did not receive it from man, nor was I taught it, but it came through a revelation of Jesus Christ... Nor did I go up to Jerusalem to those who were apostles before me...' He explains that his later visit was to talk about his mission, not to learn the gospel. That sounds like a claim to a totally independent revelation of Christianity.

Paul's authority did lie in the revelation given to him outside Damascus.

But he does not mean that Stephen, Ananias, Barnabas, and others had no part in his instruction; or that he did not subsequently learn from others many sayings of Jesus, the outline of apostolic preaching, and of elementary convert-education, the evidence for the resurrection ('what I also received', he says), the institution of the Lord's supper, the practice of baptism, and three or four of the church's hymns. His writings reveal all this. The *basis* of Paul's apostleship was that he had seen the risen Lord (1 Corinthians 9:1, 15: 8–9, Acts 1:21–22). But Paul never denied the enrichment he gained from the living church. As circumstances required, Paul could be independent and indebted, could co-operate and act alone.

A Realist Mystic?

It might seem impossible to find within one integrated personality a man of tireless action, travel, conflict, argument, strategic planning, organizing genius, and immense endurance, with a realist's awareness of the world, *and* a mystic, with intuitive insights, intense emotions, depth of thought, and constant openness to exceptional spiritual experiences. But Paul was all that.

Paul's career was marked by six clear turning-points: at Damascus, where he became a Christian; at Syrian Antioch, where he was made a missionary; near Troas, where he took the decisive step into Europe; at Corinth, which he might have left too soon, as opposition began, but where he stayed another 18 months, with marvellous results; in Jerusalem, when the end seemed near, but the crucial idea of appealing to Caesar was born (Acts 23: 11); and on board ship when 'all hope of being saved was at last abandoned', but Paul took charge. It can be shown, without exaggeration, that each of these crises was important for the gospel and for the future, as well as for Paul. *And each one was the occasion of a supernatural vision and message*, which clarified the situation, turned the scales, settled the way forward, and sustained the apostle.

It seems incredible that a man so realist in attitude, so down-to-earth in counsel, so energetic in action, so balanced and far-seeing in policy, should at the same time be a mystic, awaiting visions, listening for voices, interpreting dreams (if that is what they were), and acting in great moments upon impulses 'from beyond'. But Paul himself testifies to 'visions and revelations of the Lord... caught up to the third heaven... the abundance of revelations...'

As if aware that others would be sceptical, Paul had anticipated criticism with 'If we *are* beside ourselves, it is for God...' adding what was for him the all-sufficient explanation, 'Christ's love compels us' (NIV).

Later, a Roman governor, of no admirable character but no fool, protested at the uncomfortable directness of Paul's challenge to repentance with the cry, 'Paul, you are mad; your great learning is turning you mad'. To which Paul replied, 'I am not mad, your Excellency, I am speaking the sober truth' — which, in such company, was indeed a kind of madness.

With a man of so profound and lasting achievements, such spiritual experiences cannot be dismissed as merely psychological aberrations. The stories are told, of course, in ancient terms and definitions, but the sense of the eternal, the assurance of divine guidance, and implicit obedience to the heavenly vision, lay at the centre of Paul's motivations, however at odds it all *seems* with the man the world saw, the cities heard, the Jews feared, the Romans respected, and the Christians loved.

Nowhere in the whole wonderful story is there the least suggestion that Paul acted without thought, reason, and understanding; he listened to prophets, to colleagues, to visions, with critical mind alert, as he advised the Corinthians to do (1 Corinthians 14:29). But truth sometimes dawns directly for the waiting mind; and if we wait long enough to listen God does answer prayer. It has been suggested that Jesus, too, saw truth in pictures, instantly, 'in a flash', with visual understanding (for example Luke 4:5, 10:18).

In prayer — that elementary mystical experience which all Christians share — Paul again hardly conforms to type. He is first introduced as a Christian with the words 'Behold he is praying', and the habit of automatic recourse to God remained with him. We read of prayers which Paul offered, or shared, at Syrian Antioch, Lystra, Iconium, Pisidian Antioch, Philippi, Miletus, Tyre, and Malta, while he constantly advises others to pray watchfully, in the Spirit, and intelligently ('with the mind also'). Constantly he asks them to pray for him. Almost every letter contains a prayer for the readers, often closely appropriate to their circumstances.

Yet Paul never writes about answers to prayer. The only time he mentions 'answers' is to record that God thrice said 'No'! He never claims that '*Prayer can accomplish anything — anything at all!*'; or urges Christians to 'Wield the weapon of prayer', to 'Organize sufficient prayer', as if to coerce God; he says nothing about 'aggressive', 'positive', 'prevailing' prayer.

There is, in fact, an unexpected reticence about Paul's personal prayer-life; the only time we overhear him, he is regretting his part in Stephen's death. There is, too, a matter-of-fact quality about Paul's praying. A girl was healed at Philippi, a lad at Troas; a problem was solved; guidance was given; the storm passed. Yet Paul never says 'Prayer did it'. Paul does not believe in prayer, but in God. For Paul, prayer was simply faith made articulate; the will and power to do, or to withhold, were God's.

And Paul's faith, too, had its peculiar personal dimension. Certainly it included trust in divine assistance, providence, and protection. But no formal, systematic creed, 'Institutes of Religion', or 'Summary of Christian Theology', bears Paul's name.

The beliefs that shaped Paul's thought and strengthened his work were varied and informal. He held fast by God's sovereignty, arguing as did every Jew that all that happens must ultimately originate in the positive or the permissive will of God. Behind his own life, therefore, stood the divine purpose; he believed himself born, converted, and called, for apostleship (Galatians 1). Behind that again lay the inexplicable but unquestionable love which led Christ to give himself for Paul before Paul knew him.

When Paul mentions others of his fundamental beliefs, he frequently does so in the plural: 'We know that in everything God works for good with those who love him... That if the earthly tent we live in is destroyed, we have a building from God, eternal in the heavens... That the whole creation has been groaning in travail together until now... The grace of our Lord Jesus, that though he was rich yet for your sake he became poor, so that by his poverty you might become rich... That in the Lord your labour is not in vain... That in me, in my flesh, dwells no good thing... That the gospel is God's word that works... That love is the supreme rule of Christian life, fulfilling all divine law... That nothing in present or future, heaven or earth, life or death, can separate the earnest soul from the love of God in Christ'. These premises, for Paul, were axiomatic; supporting everything was the strong conviction that truth is invincible — 'We can do nothing against the truth, but for the truth'.

Paul Explains Himself

Yet for Paul faith was more than a grasp of truth, it was a grasp of Christ, an inner union with Christ so close, so transforming, that the man of faith 'dies' with Christ to all Christ died to, rises with Christ to victory and freedom. By accepting Christ as Saviour, a man not only says 'Yes' to Christ's dying for sin and rising again, he becomes identified with Christ in will, attitude, consent, feeling, in revulsion from sin and reaching for righteousness, and in laying hold of resurrection-life.

Paul can and does say about 240 times, that a man comes to live 'in Christ', as in a new world, a fresh atmosphere, a new universe of experience and of meaning. Or he can speak of Christ living in us, our one hope of glory.

This is how Paul himself accounts for the life he lives from day to day: 'I have been crucified with Christ; it is no longer I who live, but Christ who lives in me; and the life I now live in the flesh I live by faith in the Son of God who loved me, and gave himself for me'.

The negative — 'crucified' — aspect of Paul's life included the total surrender, to Christ's control, of freedom, thought, and action, as a purchased 'slave', bearing in his body's scars, the slave-marks that proclaimed him Christ's. It included, too, becoming a 'sacrifice' offered in rational (rather than ritual) worship, willing to be poured as libation over others' service. Supremely, Paul *loved* Christ: the only adequate analogy to Paul's relationship with Jesus was pure, enduring, selfless human love.

Paul himself hints that love for Christ may be the highest sublimation of all lesser loves (2 Corinthians 11:2,3, 1 Corinthians 7:32–35). Certainly the affective elements of Paul's nature were focused upon Jesus, not as a fading memory but as a historical figure translated now into an abiding presence.

Paul loved Christ in grateful response to Christ's love for him. He enjoyed Christ, and called on others also to 'rejoice in the Lord'. He strove to be 'worthy of the Lord, in every way pleasing' to him. For Paul, life which had begun with the apprehension of Christ, was aimed at the imitation of Christ, was sustained in union with Christ, was spent in the service of Christ, its hardships endured in the expectation of Christ.

So complete was Paul's identification with Christ that the church has long believed that Paul wrote 'to me to live *is* Christ', though the phrase is very difficult to understand. Perhaps Paul wrote 'to me to live is *chrestos*, good, and to die is gain.' Paul certainly was 'submerged' in Christ, his former self and all self-derived impulses crucified with him; old things had passed away, all things had been made new.

The positive aspect of Paul's daily life — 'Christ lives in me' — was expounded in Paul's great theme, 'the Lord is the Spirit'. Though the Spirit of God had inspired men of old, sometimes with strange results, Christians knew the Spirit as *the Spirit of Christ*, and the 'rule of the Spirit of life in Christ Jesus' was the new law of daily discipleship.　　　　　•

In over 40 passages Paul illustrates how the Spirit of Christ is active in saving, enabling, and sanctifying the Christian whose life is open towards the living Christ. This was his own experience, the invasion of his life by divine energies from outside himself, entering through faith focused upon Christ, and 'taking over', directing his activity, enlightening his understanding, equipping his ministry, renewing his resources, accumulating within his mind and heart the truth, grace, and power which constantly overflowed into other lives.

Such total and continuous dependence upon Christ, experienced as the indwelling Spirit, is the ultimate secret of this complicated man, of his achievement in the ancient world, and of his continuing influence through all the centuries since.

It is Paul's complexity that explains, in part, his wide appeal through history to followers and admirers of many kinds. For in some measure, different people find in him what they seek — the inspired thinker, the stimulating activist, the understanding brother, the wise pastor, the intriguing mystic, the strict man of discipline, the leader, the encourager, the explainer, or simply the living historic example of grace.

It is his complexity, too, that partly explains his resilience and strength. Paul only escapes becoming 'a crazy, mixed-up apostle' because he concentrated all his love upon Christ; all his thought upon the gospel; all his effort upon 'by any means, saving some'; all his ambition upon pressing toward the mark for the prize of the upward call of God in Christ Jesus. His many-sided personality found its integrity in Christ.

And that means strength. Men of Paul's calibre illustrate, not the equilibrium and serenity of adjusted poise, but the harnessing of psychological and spiritual tensions to useful and fruitful ends. Too often, our working strength is the residue left when inward conflicts have drained our energies. Paul chose the more painful way of letting his tensions generate power. His remained a far-from-placid temperament. He saw different sides of each issue, felt contrary impulses and sympathies, held to the many-sided truth, remained Jew, Roman, Christian, saved sinner and apostle, vulnerable and dedicated; and let the resulting strains kindle greater energy, and amplify his strength.

Suggestions for Group Discussion

1 Was Paul right to send a slave back to his master?

2 Did Paul, or Barnabas, contribute most to the maturing of Mark's character (Acts 15:36–41)?

3 'A foolish consistency is the hobgoblin of little minds, adored by little statesmen, philosophers, and divines' (Emerson). With Paul in mind, would the group agree?

4 Paul's 'mysticism' and 'six clear turning points' raise again the question whether there is something miraculous about *every* Christian life. Is this a needed, or a dangerous, emphasis today?

CHAPTER 4

A Fertile Correspondent

Preparatory Reading: 2 Peter 3:14–16, 2 Thessalonians 2:1–2, 3:17, Colossians 4:7–9, 2 Corinthians 10:7–11, (3:1–3).

Few historical figures are known chiefly by their correspondence, especially if the whole file could be read through on a summer afternoon. And especially if the letters were never originally meant for posterity, but written to meet local situations in the ancient world. Yet such is all we have from Paul; plus, for commentary, Luke's sadly incomplete account of some incidents in Paul's eventful life. Nevertheless, Paul's correspondence forms a lasting and powerful legacy. It is mainly as a writer that Paul continues to confront the ongoing church.

Paul's contribution to our New Testament totals less than Luke's, but includes the earliest pages to be written, before either of our gospels was issued. They provide, therefore, priceless evidence of how Jesus was remembered, and the gospel understood, over a large part of the church in the 30 years or so following Christ's ministry. But this was not their purpose. It is necessary always to remember that Paul did not address himself to our questions or situation. Paul's 'epistles' include notes to commend individuals to other Christians (Phoebe, Onesimus); answers to questions addressed to him by churches, concerning faith and conduct; responses to unwelcome news about a church; exchanges of news about churches or colleagues; appeals for help; thanks for help received; arrangements for visits; explanations of absence; encouragement, exhortations, corrections, rebukes.

The archaic name 'epistles', now used only liturgically (or facetiously), obscures the fact that these writings were simply letters, with immediate contemporary purposes. It may help to remember that they usually follow the accepted form of all private correspondence in the first century. We begin our letters with our own address, the date, the name of the addressee ('Dear...'); the message follows, with greetings and formal respect at the end, and last of all we reveal who is writing. The ancient form *began* with the writer's name, and the addressee ('A... to B...'), followed by a greeting, compliments, an acknowledgement of the gods ('Mars be praised, the war is going well...' or simply 'Honour to the divine Athena'), and possibly a prayer for the reader and family; then the message, ending with a farewell greeting, or a prayer.

Paul's 'epistles' follow this familiar pattern closely, only transposing each element into Christian terms, making the compliments, prayers, and greetings somewhat more elaborate, and directly relevant to the readers addressed. His thanksgiving to God recalls visits, and memories; his compliments concern the readers' progress in Christian life; his prayers reflect the situation of the church or individual, and often foreshadow the message that follows.

Though Paul's apostleship, his often being founder of the church addressed, and the fact that it is a letter to a church as a whole, lends a certain formal tone to the instruction, counsel, or rebuke conveyed, the form leaves no doubt that it is a personal letter, not a sermon or treatise.

For delivery, Paul employed the couriers available, Timothy, Tychicus, Titus or others (see Colossians 4:7–9, Ephesians 6:21–22), and the messenger would usually be present when the letter was read, to explain or supplement its contents.

It follows that, before we attempt to interpret Paul's correspondence, we must investigate the circumstances behind each letter. We must remember, too, that the letters usually follow Paul's visits, and passages we find obscure would be easily understood by those familiar with the writer's preaching.

No one letter, nor all together, set forth the whole of Paul's teaching, even on one subject; they recall, re-emphasize, apply, or supplement, what Paul has already taught. The apostle was concerned always with people and their problems, never with merely academic issues; and each letter shows, not the whole Paul but Paul faced with some particular question, circumstance, criticism or danger. In spite of this contemporary relevance, Paul's letters do contain, of course, insights, counsel, teaching, and outstanding passages, that are unquestionably timeless.

Preservation
The Corinthian church thought Paul's letters 'weighty and strong'; the Roman church might have agreed with 'weighty'; the Galatians would agree with 'strong'. In 2 Peter 3:15–16 we read, in connection with God's forbearance in delaying the End-time, 'So also our beloved Paul wrote to you according to the wisdom given him, speaking of this as he does in all his letters. There are some things in them hard to understand, which the ignorant and unstable twist to their own destruction, as they do the other scriptures'. This is high, if guarded praise. Already (late first century?) Paul's writing is classed with other 'scriptures', and cited in support of what is being

taught. Already, too, 'some things are hard to understand', probably because the original circumstances and context were fading from memory.

'All his letters' suggest that the readers knew of correspondence not originally addressed to themselves, implying some circulation, or even a collection, of Paul's letters. At first, each church would keep what Paul wrote to themselves, or some of it, and we are almost compelled to conclude that sometimes for safety's sake, or for economy, they copied on to one papyrus more than one letter, or note. Limited circulation began even during Paul's lifetime, for he asked Laodicea and Colossae to exchange letters (Colossians 4:16). This providing of copies for other churches also led to copying different letters on single papyri.

Early Christian literature shows that circulation and collection of the precious utterances of the early leaders developed with the passing of the apostolic age, and the beginning of the second century. There is reason to believe that a bishop in Ephesus, about AD 100, collected all the copies of Paul's letters available to him, to make one parchment roll. His name was Onesimus, and he was quite possibly the runaway slave whom Paul converted and returned to Philemon.

Such collecting began the production of our New Testament. The order of the letters varied in different collections; those to the same church were eventually kept together, the longest being placed first; and those to churches were placed before those to individuals. The order of writing, therefore, has to be discovered, if possible, from the contents.

Not all of Paul's correspondence was preserved, however. He wrote one letter to Corinth before our *1 Corinthians* (1 Corinthians 5:9); whether any part of it has survived is debatable. Paul also apparently wrote *to* Laodicea (Colossians 4:16); it is less likely that Paul would commend a letter written *from* the Laodicean church. No authentic 'Paul to the Laodiceans' now exists. A composition of Pauline texts, with that title, was canvassed in the church for some 900 years, but it was too obviously a fabrication to be taken seriously. One early writer thought Paul was referring to our *Ephesians*. How many other authentic writings of Paul never survived, we cannot know of course.

Cautions — Is It Paul's?

Two dangers immediately become apparent. One is of deliberate 'forgery', though that may be too strong a word if the motive was innocent. No question of personal gain, or of infringed 'copyright' arises, nor even of falsehood, in ascribing a 'letter' or 'treatise' to an honoured teacher, unless some false teaching is thus given spurious authority.

However strange it may appear to us, the issue of religious documents under assumed names, for innocent reasons *did* occur. Paul himself warned the church at Thessalonica against being 'quickly shaken in mind or excited, either by spirit or by word, or by letter purporting to be from us...' If such warning were needed while Paul lived, how much more after his death, when someone with special interest, for example, in the coming advent wished to record and circulate what Paul had taught on that subject; or when a devoted disciple wished to recall Paul's principles and apply them to a later situation. Neither would wish to pass off the teaching as his own: in all sincerity, he would be anxious that the truth he preserved should be recognized as a summary, or an application, of his master's insights.

An 'epistle of Christ', gospels by Philip, Thomas, 'the Hebrews', Nicodemus, 'Acts' of John, Peter, Andrew, Thomas, Barnabas, and 'Apocalypses' of Peter, Paul, Thomas, Stephen, and others, leave us no alternative but to reckon with this custom. Not all were from orthodox, or pious, motives. Little of this kind attributed to Paul has survived, except the 'epistle to Laodicea', six short letters supposed to have been written to the Roman philosopher-statesman Seneca, and a few fragments. Usually they consist of verses culled from existing letters, or are wholly unlike Paul's writing. It is plainly unnecessary to accept as Paul's all that is attributed to him, even by name, but with skill and honest judgement to examine the thought, methods of argument, style, date, and supposed circumstances, comparing each point with letters known to be authentic.

The other danger is that documents whose authorship was not known, or suppressed, might be attributed to Paul, just as our four anonymous gospels, *Acts, 1, 2, 3 'John'* came to be attributed to the authors whose names they now bear. The outstanding instance of traditional attribution to Paul is the magnificent and anonymous *epistle to the Hebrews*. Some in the early church seem to have felt that only Paul *could* have written this splendid sustained argument, although Origen, the greatest biblical scholar of the early third century, declared that only God knew who wrote it.

The difficulties in accepting it as Paul's are almost insuperable. True, the epistle uses great Pauline words like 'faith', 'sanctified', 'perfect', 'law', but in ways quite different from Paul's — one could not possibly (for example) read Hebrews 11 giving Paul's meaning to the word 'faith'.

Hebrews betrays a second-generation author by speaking of the gospel as 'attested unto us by those who heard Jesus'; Paul claimed to have seen the Lord, and received his gospel directly from him. *Hebrews'* whole argument, about the Mosaic Tabernacle ritual, about Christianity fulfilling and so preserving all that was important in Judaism, is totally different from the way Paul deals with the relation of Christianity to Judaism. Its use of the Old

Testament is different from Paul's too; nor, as far as we know, did Paul write anything else anonymously. Most of Paul's ruling ideas — justification by faith-union with Christ; the church, the body of Christ, the unity of Jew and Gentile, the sacraments, the coming advent of Christ, the ethical teaching of Jesus, and, strangest of all, the Holy Spirit (hardly mentioned) — find no place in *Hebrews.*

To write *Hebrews*, Paul must have changed not only his language but the basis of his Christian thinking. On the other side, there is nothing to urge but tentative and late church tradition. We may be grateful that not knowing the name of the author does not affect our appreciation of this argument for going on with Christ. The question is probably the most fascinating of all the unsolved puzzles of the New Testament; one attractive (and defensible) guess may be that *Hebrews* was written by Priscilla.

When we compare disputed writings attributed to Paul with those generally believed to be his, one caution arises from the method of Paul's writing. We know that he suffered from impaired sight (Galatians 4:13–15, Acts 23: 2–5, 9:8–9,18), and that he employed Tertius to write Romans 16. He says plainly, at the end of *1 Corinthians, Galatians, Colossians, 2 Thessalonians*, that he has taken the pen into his own hand to close each epistle.

It was obviously Paul's habit to use secretaries. Silas (Silvanus) joined Paul in writing *1 and 2 Thessalonians*; he also helped with *1 Peter* (5:12), which suggests that he may have been one of a numerous class of trained copyists, or scribes. In *Galatians*, having recalled his poor sight, Paul adds, 'See with what large letters I am writing...'; in *2 Thessalonians*, where he had referred to letters 'purporting' to be from him, he says 'I, Paul, write this greeting with my own hand. This is the mark in every letter of mine; it is the way I write'.

This implies that Paul *dictated* his letters. If we recall that they were also intended to be read aloud to groups assembled for worship, many of whom would be illiterate, we shall appreciate better the eloquent 'preaching' tone of many passages. And experiment will show that reading aloud, as to an audience, often clarifies closely argued passages. Moreover, dictation tends to encourage digression, especially for a rich, 'overflowing' mind accustomed to preaching.

Paul sometimes permits himself a side-glance at some train of thought related to his immediate theme. He also sometimes interrupts himself, even corrects himself, as his spoken thought hurries on. And still more often he anticipates what he plans to say later, letting an argument or an appeal 'slip out' too soon, and returning to it again in its place — as preachers often do. (For examples: side-glance at related thoughts — 1 Corinthians 3:16–17, 9:21, 11:11,12; self-interruption — Galatians 2:4,5 and 6, 2 Corinthians 11:23, Ephesians 3:1,14; self-correction — Romans 1:11–12, 1 Corinthians

10:28–29; anticipation — Romans 3:1–2 resumed at 9:4–5, 1 Corinthians 6:12–13 resumed at 10:23–24, 3:16–17 resumed in new connection at 6:19–20.)

Paul's use of secretaries also warns us that we must use arguments about Paul's 'literary style' with due care. Much will depend upon how detailed Paul's dictation was. In passages where precise statement was important, the scribe might reproduce Paul's exact words; at other points Paul might well say, 'Give them my earnest greetings, and tell them I hope to visit them', leaving the precise wording to the scribe. (Paul closes letters four times with a reference to the 'holy kiss'; the only other reference is in 1 Peter, which one of Paul's secretaries penned. Is it, then, a 'secretarial' touch?) We must not be too confident that *every* word is Paul's own; computer-counting can be misleading.

The Pauline 'Style'

Sufficient similarity, however, marks Paul's undisputed letters for us to speak in general of Paul's 'style'. Or, more accurately, of his several styles, preaching, debating, rabbinic, and informal (as in *Philemon*). He can be vehement and stormy, as in *Galatians*; aggressive, rapier-like, as in later chapters of *2 Corinthians*; tender and heart-moving as in 1 Corinthians 13; winsome as in *Philemon*; didactic as in *1 Corinthians*; logical and lawyer-like as in *Romans*; pastoral as in *1 Thessalonians*, and still be unmistakably Paul. He coins words to express new meanings, and sometimes stretches syntax somewhat irregularly, adapting Greek with equal readiness to Old Testament ways of speech, to argument, to eloquence, and to song.

Paul's word-coinage is always stimulating. Beside the 'fellow-soldier, fellow-sufferer, fellow-labourer' group, is one almost as large coined with the Greek equivalent of 'super', which could only pass into elegant English as '*more than* conquerors', 'more than grow', 'more than overflow', 'more than outshine' and the rest. (The Greek syllable is '*hyper*', as appropriately in 'hyperbole'.)

At one point Paul's skill falters, in the use of illustrations and analogies. The analogy proposed in Romans 7:1–4 is the freedom of the living widow from the marriage-law following her husband's death, but it is the freedom of the *dead* that is argued in 4–6. In Romans 5:12–19, Paul aims both to compare and to contrast Christ and Adam, simultaneously. And no one is sure just what Paul was seeking to 'illustrate' by his analogy of Sarah, Hagar, Sinai, Jerusalem, in Galatians 4:21–31! Paul's thought so often outruns his metaphors.

Classical scholars have often spoken appreciatively of Paul's writing. 'Here, if anywhere, the style is the man . . . We have to realize that Paul is one of the great writers of Greece and of the world. He has a great range of living allusion and metaphor. The flaming individuality of his mind is through all his style, in the tangents... the hyperbole... his superlatives... a series of explosions... his amazing vocabulary... the compressed word-pictures... the popular phrase... the Septuagint echoes... (Dr T. R. Glover, Cambridge).

And E. Norden (referring to a foremost Greek stylist of 300–220 BC) says, 'In Paul the language of the heart is born again. Since the hymn of Cleanthes, nothing so intimate, nothing so splendid, had been written as Paul's hymn to love. Those two hymns, of love to God and love to men (Romans 8:31–39, 1 Corinthians 13) have given again to the Greek language what had been lost for centuries, the intimacy and the enthusiasm of the mystic'.

And Dr C. H. Dodd remarked that Paul could declaim upon the vices of the age like a satirist, speculate upon God and conscience like a philosopher, argue from scripture like a rabbi, analyze experience like a psychologist, and view the universe (in Romans 8) with the vision of a poet.

Paul's letters are obviously worthy of study. Yet, of course, it is not for his literary craftsmanship that thousands have turned to Paul with reverence, love, and gratitude, feeling in him the divine inspiration that imparts truth, encouragement, and life. It is astonishing that such short letters, hastily, often urgently, penned could enshrine such intensity of thought and spiritual power, to nourish generations of Christians, shape the philosophical (and even much political) thinking of the western world, and provide a standard by which the teaching of the church in every age has been tested and kept true.

Paul's little file of correspondence is still treasured across the modern world as a supreme expression of the Christian faith, an irreplaceable interpretation of Jesus, an armoury from which weapons have been drawn to fight distortion and heresy, a burning bush at which innumerable torches have been kindled, an unfailing spring of spiritual refreshment and power.

Suggestions for Group Discussion

1 Modern Christians are linked with the Christian beginnings by a continuous living fellowship, a ritual, and a book (church, sacrament, testament): which is the most important? Could the church survive without them?

2 The New Testament came into being in strangely 'haphazard' fashion, as each writer responded to his contemporary situation without thought of writing for posterity. What does this imply for the way we interpret and use it?

3 Ask two members to prepare to speak, one for and one against modern translations of the Bible. Then discuss the advantages and disadvantages.

4 Ask members of the group to read aloud his/her favourite passage from Paul — consider: Romans 8:31–39; 1 Corinthians 15:21–28, 35–44, 51–58; Philippians 2:1–11; 1 Thessalonians 4:13–18; 2 Corinthians 4; and 5:11–21 and so on.

CHAPTER 5

The Galatian Outburst

Preparatory Reading: Acts 13:51–14:23, Galatians 1, 3:1–5, 4:1–20, 5:13–25, ch. 6

Almost the first noticeable thing about Paul's letter to the Galatians is the absence of all personal greetings, of the customary compliments, good wishes, names of individuals remembered with affection or gratitude: it is addressed baldly to 'the churches of Galatia'. If we seek a kindly farewell greeting at the end, all we find is 'Henceforth let no man trouble me...' and the brief 'grace'.

Even more surprising is the absence of thoughtful prayer for the readers. Instead, a somewhat formal 'grace to you and peace from God... and our Lord Jesus Christ... to whom be glory...' is followed at once by 'I am astonished that you are so quickly deserting him who called you...'

The listening congregation must have sat up straight, disturbed at so curt an opening. But the tone sharpens with each paragraph. 'I am astonished at you...' leads to 'Am I seeking favours of you?'... 'I would have you know, brethren...'... 'O foolish Galatians, who has bewitched you?'... 'Tell me, you who want to be under law...'... 'Now I, Paul, say to you...'...'Do not be fooled...'

In 4:11 Paul actually suggests that coming to Galatia at all might prove to have been a dead loss! It is all so vehement, vigorous, blunt, militant. There are gentler paragraph-openings, for Paul is not angry with them all; but the explosive phrases remain. And Paul knows that his tone is wrong: 'I could wish to be present with you now and to change my tone, for I am perplexed about you'.

It is not only the language that is harsh. Paul twice pronounces a solemn curse upon certain opponents (1:8–9), adding later, more soberly, 'he who is troubling you will bear his judgement, whoever he is!' He declares that his opponents are hindering the work of Christ; they are not of God. He challenges their falsity, their slyness (2:4), their self-seeking and self-importance (4:17), their insincerity and cowardice (6:12–13).

Paul's vehemence overflows in disrespect against even the leaders of the Jerusalem church: 'From those... reputed to be something (what they were makes no difference to me; God shows no partiality), those I say who were of repute added nothing to me...'

Again: 'When Cephas came to Antioch I opposed him to his face, because he stood condemned... with him the rest of the Jews acted insincerely... they were not straightforward about the truth of the gospel...' And one very harsh, even coarse, expression in 5:12 exaggerates circumcision into self-castration; even NEB, in a beautiful English accent, disguises it as 'these agitators, they had better go the whole way and make eunuchs of themselves'.

Plainly, Paul is angry, and the spectacle of an apostle in a passion commands attention.

The first hint as to what has upset Paul arises when we identify 'Galatia'. After long and learned discussion of some ambiguous regional names used by Luke, it is widely accepted that Paul is addressing the churches of Iconium, Lystra, Derbe, and any daughter-churches in the surrounding country. Galatia was a Roman province in mid-Asia Minor and extending northwards; argument has mainly concerned how far north Paul had travelled, and whether his letter was addressed to a more northerly region — of which, in fact, we know very little.

The story of Paul's adventurous evangelization of the Iconium area is told in Acts 13:51–14:23, where the mixed Jewish-Gentile congregation at Iconium, and even more the references to pagan worship at Lystra, at once indicate the Galatian problem: the right relationship of Jews and Gentiles in the church of Christ. Paul had suffered badly at the hands of Jewish opponents on his first visit: everything in *Galatians* confirms that the trouble was continuing within the churches, and that this was the occasion of writing. Together with early citations of the letter, this correspondence of letter and story leaves no doubt the epistle is Paul's.

The Story

Until Paul had set out with Barnabas from Syrian Antioch on his first missionary journey, the church had consisted almost entirely of Christian Jews. The conversion of an Ethiopian, of certain Samaritans, of the Roman Cornelius, and then of a number of Syrians at Antioch, had seriously disturbed the mother-church at Jerusalem, and raised the divisive question, '*On what terms* should Gentiles be admitted to Christ's church, the "Christian sect" of Judaism'? While this remained unsettled, a Roman official was converted by Paul on Cyprus, and soon afterwards Paul's mission was extended to Pamphylia in Asia Minor, and Galatia, moving deliberately beyond the synagogue audiences and offering to Gentiles salvation by faith in Christ alone, with considerable success.

When Paul reported this to the home-church at Syrian Antioch, the simmering disagreements came to a head. A solemn council was held at Jerusalem, which decreed that Jews and Gentiles alike were saved by faith in Christ, and no Jewish yoke, *such as demands for circumcision,* food taboos, the Mosaic law, other than obvious pious duties, was to be laid upon Gentile converts. The terms of the decree leave no question that some unauthorized Jewish Christians had already made such demands, unsettling the minds of Gentile Christians (see Acts 15).

(According to Acts 9:26, 11:30, 15:2, Paul visited Jerusalem (after his conversion) *three* times, but in *Galatians* Paul mentions only *two* visits, saying nothing of the Jerusalem council, nor of the decree there promulgated, which so intimately concerned the Galatian converts. This seems to require that Paul wrote Galatians before the council met, about AD 49, making it the earliest of Paul's letters, and the beginning of our New Testament. It must be admitted that there are some difficulties of detail in harmonizing all that Paul says with what Luke records — probably arising from our incomplete knowledge. Speaking of visiting Galatia, in 4:13, Paul uses a phrase which is translated ('I visited you...') 'at the first' (AV/KJV), 'at first' (RSV), 'originally' (NEB), 'I first preached' (NIV), but 'formerly, on the first of my two visits' in NEB margin. If, however, Paul is writing after two visits to Galatia (that is, after his second mission journey) it is very difficult to explain why he did not mention *three* visits to Jerusalem, and the council's decree on the issue under discussion. Here also a long and learned discussion has ensued, but more recently opinion has tended to fix on the earlier date, before the council, placing Galatians in the midst of the rising agitation about the terms of Gentile salvation.)

Those jealous for the ancient and sacred traditions of Judaism, could not see, as Paul saw so clearly, that habits of piety and rituals of observance which may be profitable to some Christians, enshrining their early training and first experiences of God, may have no value at all for other Christians with different backgrounds.

One especially painful issue concerned table-fellowship with Gentiles, which strict Jews avoided at all costs, partly because Gentile food would often be 'unclean' to Jews, partly because by eastern custom shared meals implied friendship and loyalty. Thus, to share the Lord's Table with Christians who were not accepted converts to Judaism was a serious breach of Jewish etiquette and respectability (see Acts 11:2–3).

More important than pious custom was the sacred, unalterable divine law, obedience to which merited salvation; disobedience (when Jews ruled their own land) was a capital crime. To deny this was blasphemous — and perilous. In a sinful world, law alone could keep order: Romans and Greeks knew this as clearly as Jews. Gentiles, lacking divine law (as Jews held) were naturally idolatrous, sensual, materialistic, sexually undisciplined.

Bitter experience had taught Jews the moral peril of Gentile influence; under Greek rule the Maccabeans, and under Roman rule the Pharisees, had fiercely resisted the inroads of paganism, by insisting upon the supremacy of the divine law. When Jews spoke of freedom (from foreign domination, through Messiah, for example) they always assumed that freedom would be kept safe for society by total subservience to God's law. Christian Jews could appeal also to the words and example of Jesus to prove that God's law *must* be observed.

To offer the lawless Gentiles salvation by faith in Christ, alone, was to open the church's doors to every kind of excess, immorality, vice, disunity. Faith alone would not civilize Gentiles: moral restraint was essential, and Gentile converts must accept the law that God gave through Moses, as well as forgiveness through Christ, if their 'salvation' was to be safe. Paul must have misunderstood the gospel. A renegade to his old faith, who had never walked with Jesus listening to the authentic word, and therefore no true apostle, Paul had learned the gospel secondhand — and got it wrong!

The hint in the Jerusalem council's decree that teachers claiming authority from the mother-church had troubled Gentile converts with Judaist demands, is confirmed by the emergence at Corinth of a 'Peter party' opposing Paul (1 Corinthians 1:12, 3:22), and similar trouble perhaps at Philippi (Philippians 3:2–11).

It seems that such emissaries from the Jerusalem circle were following Paul, seeking to 'correct' his teaching. In Galatia, some prominent individual (1:8–9, 5:10), with a supporting group (1:7, 4:17, 5:12 'agitators' NEB, 6:12) had accepted this Judaist version of the gospel, and were requiring circumcision of the Galatians (5:2,6, 6:3), the observance of traditional festivals (4:10), and above all obedience of the Mosaic law (3:2,5,10–14, 4:21). Paul resisted these demands, as a return to childhood's elementary religious ideas (4:3,9 NIV), as meaningless for Gentiles (3:6–9), as making Christ unnecessary (2:21, 5:2–4), and as seriously limiting the freedom which Christ's redemption conferred (5:1).

This is a consistent and persuasive reading of the scattered descriptions of those who were 'troubling' the Galatians. Some verses can be differently read. RSV speaks of Paul and the Galatians as formerly 'slaves to the elemental spirits of the universe', and the Galatians turning back to 'the weak and beggarly elemental spirits whose slaves you want to be once more'. NEB translates similarly, but with margin 'the elements of the natural world' or 'elementary ideas belonging to this world'. NIV offers, 'basic principles of the world . . . those weak and miserable principles' (4:3,9).

Taken with hints of astrology, (4:10); licentiousness (5:16–21, 6:7–8); and claims to superior spirituality, and to 'know God', 4:8–9, 6:1, these renderings suggest that 'gnostic' ideas, such as certainly affected nearby Colossae, had also reached Galatia. This is clearly possible. But the basic 'gnostic' idea — salvation by knowledge, *gnosis* — is absent; the reference to licentiousness in contrast with the fruits of the Spirit, to the festivals, and to arrogant spirituality, are perfectly understandable without this assumption. Moreover Paul does not here offer any anti-gnostic argument.

The Message

Such was the debate disturbing Galatia, and as soon as Paul heard of it he dashed off his first, and most fiery pastoral letter. He announces himself at once as an apostle by divine appointment, and quickly launches into a strong defence of the gospel he preached, authenticated by Christ in his own experience. Commissioned so to preach, he had conferred with no human authority, but took time to think things through. It was three years before he visited Jerusalem privately to see the president of the church, the Lord's own brother. And another 14 years before he went again, by divine leading, to explain his mission. No issue about circumcision was then raised — a few sly people tried, but Paul resisted. The outcome was an agreed division of spheres. (There Paul drops discussion of his own status; the issues must be argued from principles, not personalities.)

Unfortunately this harmony did not last. When Peter visited Syrian Antioch, he and others refused to eat with Gentile Christians lest they offend strict Jews. Paul had strongly opposed the implied inconsistency. Retelling this, Paul anticipates his main argument: 'as Jews ourselves, we have found that no one is counted righteous by keeping the law, but only on the ground of faith'. If it turns out that even so we are sinners, that does not prove Christ promotes sin, but only that we are inconsistent. In fact, Paul continues, through the law I died, crucified with Christ, and live now by faith in Christ. We do not deny God's grace; but if any is righteous through keeping the law, then Christ died for nothing.

Turning to appeal, Paul asks his 'foolish Galatians' who had bewitched them; how had they originally received the Spirit, by law-keeping, or by faith? Scripture is clear: by reckoning Abraham's faith as righteousness, God preached salvation by faith to all nations. The law can only curse, it is faith that brings life. Christ loosed us all from the curse of the law that Abraham's blessing might come to Gentiles who share his faith, and with it the promise of the Spirit, an inheritance originating in promise, not in the much later law.

Certainly the law curbs transgression. Before faith in Christ was possible, law was the guardian of our childhood; now, in Christ, we have attained sonship, and as sons we are no longer Jew, Greek, slave, freeman, male, female, but all *one*. Because you Gentiles are Christ's you are, already, Abraham's descendants and heirs. We have had our childhood period of subservience, like slaves: now God has sent his Son, and the Spirit of his Son into our hearts, *setting us free* from law to call God 'Father' and inherit blessing. For the Galatians now to return to immaturity and re-enter bondage would undo all Paul's work.

In moving remembrance of his welcome in Galatia, Paul pleads for the Galatians' loyalty, their love in return for his; then he quickly resumes argument, basing the new freedom of the Christian upon a confused rabbinic-style analogy concerning Hagar and Sarah, to show that Christians are born free. Above all, therefore, Christians must preserve that Christ-given freedom, refusing to return to slavery. To accept circumcision is to make Christ of no advantage, to fall from grace back to legalism, obliged to observe *all* the law.

Whereas it is by the Spirit, not by the law, that we can hope to attain righteousness; the Spirit received through faith — and that is all that matters, faith working through love, in the power of the Spirit. Why do not the Galatians see this — they were doing so well! If Paul preaches circumcision (as some seem to have reported) why should he be persecuted by the Jews? The offence of the cross would be cancelled, too. And impatiently he dismisses the question.

For Christ's call was to freedom — not to license, but to freedom in love and service. Walking in the Spirit curbs the flesh; being led by the Spirit frees from law; to bear the fruits of the Spirit is to live above all law. To walk in the Spirit is to crucify sensual desire, and live without conceit, provocation, envy. When any man falls, the man of the Spirit will restore him gently, watchful of himself. So he will fulfil the only law still binding — Christ's law of love. But let not any be boastful: each must carry his own responsibility. Let the taught share with the teacher in all good things, remembering that in all well-doing we reap as generously or sparingly as we sow.

Taking up the pen, Paul warns against insincere, self-serving teachers. Paul will boast only in the cross. He repeats that neither circumcision nor uncircumcision counts for anything, but only new creation in Christ. May peace rest on all who accept that rule, the true Israel of God. As for his own status, let no one trouble him again, he bears Christ's slave-marks. A brief closing grace.

Gathering Paul's main arguments into concise summary reveals their force. Faith, not law, saved the Galatians, as Abraham himself was saved; law can curse, but not save; God's gracious covenant rested on promise and faith, not the later law; and looked towards Christ. Law is useful for training children, but we are sons, heirs, freeborn; the choice is between saving oneself by keeping the law, or being saved by Christ through faith: we cannot have both. The Spirit will fulfil in us all the law that matters — the law of love, but a man can be open to the Spirit's rule only if he is free from all other regulations. So: no circumcision, no bondage, no law, only faith, freedom, and life in the Spirit.

If we gather also Paul's 16 references in *Galatians'* 149 verses (one every nine verses) to the Spirit, we shall understand Paul's fundamental concern. The Galatians had begun with the Spirit; Christ redeemed us that we might receive the promise of the Spirit, the Spirit of God's Son; we are born 'according to the Spirit', and through the Spirit we wait for the hope of righteousness. Therefore we must walk by the Spirit, be led by the Spirit, bear the fruit of the Spirit, live in the Spirit. He who thus sows to the Spirit shall reap eternal life.

Though brief and argumentative, and somewhat deranged by emotion, this description of the individual Christian's experience of the holy Spirit deserves to be placed alongside that in Romans 8, and that of the church's corporate experience in 1 Corinthians 12–14. *This is Paul's answer to those following Jewish customs or rites: not the law but the Spirit rules the Christian life*, preserving him from all viciousness, enabling him for all good. The Christian lives by inward guidance, not outward compulsion; by inspiration, not regulation; by shining insights and flexible principles, and not by ancient commandments.

Enduring Relevance

Even summarized and smoothed, Paul's Galatian outburst remains almost incoherent with indignation. Did the issue of faith versus law matter so very much? Paul would certainly reply that it did. A man must either trust for his salvation in what Christ did for him, or in his own efforts; only the former is Christianity. Besides, lives held in legal bondage must fail to respond to the prompting of Christ's free Spirit.

Even so, were Paul's verbal fireworks justified? Again Paul would say 'Yes'. He was fighting three battles at once — that of the Galatians, against those who hindered, bewitched, confused and disturbed young converts; his own, too, for the argument challenged not only his apostleship but his own spiritual experience and work; and Christianity's battle, to break free from Judaism and become a world faith. With so much at stake, Paul could not possibly compromise.

Racial and cultural barriers confront Christianity still. *Galatians* is Paul's timeless contribution to the long debate about the inter-racial dimension of the gospel. Christianity's independence of any racial, national, local or traditional cultural pattern is here established. God had not left himself without witness among Gentiles any more than among Jews; the gospel fulfils and completes whatever of the truth men have already glimpsed, whatever they 'ignorantly worship'. In Christ there *is* neither Jew nor Greek, slave nor free, male nor female, black, coloured, 'white' or yellow, Caucasian, Semitic, Negroid, Mongol, Aborigine, Asian, Polynesian, Arab — or other. In Christ Jesus all are one.

The problem of freedom, likewise, confronts both church and society still, and *Galatians* offers a remarkable dissertation upon its nature and limits. Paul glances successively at freedom from law, from dependence upon man, from the curse of guilt, from the restraints of childhood, from the slavery of the flesh. In no sense is Paul thinking of mere irresponsibility, or rebelliousness; Christians enjoy the liberty of those born free, redeemed from slavery, grown mature, citizens of heaven, and rescued from ignorance and superstition.

Even while urging Christians to stand fast in this manifold liberty conferred by Christ, Paul diverges widely from modern libertarian assumptions. The freedom he cherishes is far from self-will asserting itself against all restraint; it is exercised within loyalties and obligations, freely accepted, that limit, enrich, and undergird it. Paul mentions, again successively:

- loyalty to the true gospel — no one is free to distort the truth
- loyalty to the divine commission — the Christian is not free to desert his vocation
- loyalty to moral integrity — inconsistency is not freedom
- loyalty to self-discipline — license is not liberty, either
- loyalty to social responsibility and love — Christians can never be free of each other
- loyalty to Christ, whose law is supreme.

Such limitations are not burdensome to hearts in love with Christ: they remain binding, nevertheless, adding to the security and value of the freedom with which Christ has made us free.

And the promise of the Spirit still confronts the church, and the Christian. But a man must be free from the past and its dead tradition, from his own slaveries, from fear of men and the pressures of society, from the tyranny of the State, if he is to be responsive to the Spirit's sway, open to the Spirit's prompting, teachable under the Spirit's instruction, unobstructive to the Spirit's power. The great danger of a return to Jewish legalism was rigidity of mind, that could not hear God's new word in Jesus, and inflexibility of will, that could not bend to God's new purposes.

That warning is never out of date. The temptation of the church is ever to fear liberty, to channel inspiration into organization, to tame the prophets, discipline the saints, legalize morals, and formularize the faith. That is why Luther, *with Galatians in his hand*, addressed the church in Europe 'Concerning Christian Liberty'. Order is essential: but so is freedom to follow the leading of Christ's Spirit into new truth, new enterprise, new problems, and each new age.

Suggestions for Group Discussion

1 Paul held that the attempt to make Gentiles become good Jews before they could become Christians was all wrong: should we try to make 'foreign' Christians become good Westerners, democrats, Anglicans/Episcopalians/Presbyterians/Methodists/Baptists/ Roman Catholics (and so on)? How much is *essential* in making new Christians?

2 The first Christians came to Christianity via Judaism and the Old Testament; do all Christians have to come that way? Or should every native pre-Christian faith be similarly regarded as leading up to fuller revelation in Christ? Is Acts 17:22–31 relevant here?

3 Freedom always brings problems, in home, church, society, and the State. Jews tried to safeguard freedom by law; Greeks by moderation in all things; Romans by citizenship and discipline; the church by canon law, scripture, tradition, convention. Paul lists six limits to Christian freedom, beside the rule of the Spirit. Is any freedom left? — enough here for any alert group to discuss!

CHAPTER 6

Comforting the Thessalonians

Preparatory Reading; Acts 17:1–15, 1 Thessalonians, 2 Thessalonians 3

Paul vividly remembered his visit to Thessalonica, an ancient Macedonian city on the main road from the east to Rome, and capital of its province. He recalls with warm thanksgiving the power and conviction of his mission there, and how readily and completely many turned from idolatry to serve a living God. Ill-treatment at Philippi had not discouraged the missionary party; their motives were obviously sincere, their manner gentle and affectionate (Paul recalls), and they had 'worked night and day' to maintain themselves, not to be burdensome to the converts. The resulting enthusiasm of the Thessalonians had fully rewarded all.

Luke's summary of the same events adds that the mission began with three sabbath's preaching in the synagogue, winning some Jews and a great many of the Gentile 'God fearers' attending the services, with 'not a few' leading women of the city.

Such success stirred jealousy among the unbelieving Jews, who created uproar, and accused Jason (the apostles' host) and some other Christians of subverting Roman rule. The city authorities released the accused on surety of good behaviour, and Paul and Silas were at once sent on to Beroea, some 60 miles (95 kilometres) away. When Thessalonian Jews pursued Paul there, he was again sent forward, with companions, to Athens, leaving Silas and Timothy behind. The returning escort were instructed to send Silas and Timothy to Paul, who awaited them at Athens (Acts 17:15–16). The date was about AD 49–50.

The 'great many' Gentile converts suggests a longer mission than three weeks. So does the repeated help which Paul received from Philippi (Philippians 4:16) — in spite of 'working night and day'. Luke has evidently telescoped the story, to concentrate upon Athens and Corinth. But his picture of real success at Thessalonica rousing sharp opposition confirms Paul's account. Luke adds that Silas and Timothy caught up with Paul at *Corinth*; 1 Thessalonians 1:1 shows that both were with Paul when that epistle was written. Paul, however, in the longer of his two letters (1 Thessalonians 3:1–6) reveals that Timothy at any rate rejoined him at *Athens*, only to be sent back from there to establish and comfort the Thessalonians under continuing persecution. How long he stayed we do not know, nor whether his return with 'good news' was from this visit, as seems probable, or possibly a later one.

After visiting Palestine from Corinth, Paul returned westwards to Ephesus, staying for two-to-three years, and then revisited Macedonia some five-to-six years after the first visit. Luke's phrase 'through these parts' suggests that Thessalonica would have been included in this tour, especially as when Paul went again to Jerusalem, to deliver gifts, he took Aristarchus and Secundus of Thessalonica with him (Acts 20:4).

Order of Writing

Where our two epistles fit into this story must be gathered from their contents. It can scarcely be doubted that some considerable time elapsed between Paul's first visit and his writing the longer letter. By that time, the reputation of the Macedonian church has reached not only all Macedonia but also Achaia (southern Greece). Enough members of the church have died to raise sad and perplexed questioning about how such may fare at the Lord's coming (4:13–18). Persecution has subsided somewhat (2:14 'you *suffered*'), and is looked back upon (3:4).

There is, too, a distinctly defensive note in the long explanation, affectionate remembrances, regret at not being able to revisit Thessalonica, which suggests sufficient time has passed for some criticism to arise at Paul's long absence. Paul labours this apology in a way that implies the Thessalonians had some cause for complaint: 'we endeavoured the more eagerly and with great desire to see you face to face ... We wanted to come to you, I, Paul, again and again, but Satan hindered us'. (Paul presumably wrote this before the vision of Christ commanded him to stay at Corinth — Acts 18:9).

In this longer epistle, the exhortation to quiet work and orderly daily life (4:11–12) is summarily recalled, as something familiar to the readers, not now urgent. It seems unlikely, too, that three chapters of reminiscence would be required if Paul had only recently left Thessalonica. Some have thought that the repeated exhortation to 'respect' and 'esteem' their leaders, and 'be at peace among themselves', requires more organization than Paul could probably arrange during a brief and stormy first visit.

More plausibly, perhaps, it is suggested that some disaffection had arisen, evidence of a slackening of zeal and cooling of united joy. The solemn charge that this letter be read openly to all the brethren, not reserved to some small clique, or to the leaders, reinforces this suggestion. The detailed recalling of earlier zest and joy would also, then, have greater significance.

For so short a letter, so many hints of the passage of time, inconclusive though each is when taken alone, amount to a firm impression that the longer Thessalonian letter looks back some way to the original mission.

In contrast, such time-notes as there are in the very brief 'shorter epistle' show that it was written while persecution was at its height (1:4–10), and when Paul could speak with warmth of the way the Thessalonians' faith was growing and their love increasing, as one might do to new converts with less risk of offence. The thrice-repeated note of command, too, might be more acceptable to new Christians than to a church already critical and disaffected. Again, Paul urges that they shall not be 'quickly' shaken in mind about Christ's advent, meaning apparently 'so soon after our teaching you' (2:1–2,5). Paul has confidence that their early zeal continues (3:4). He recalls his teaching and example while with them, on a single point, rather than rehearsing the whole story of his mission (3:6–12). While the exhortation to work in quietness and independence is here spelled out, rather than summarized.

At the end, Paul explains that it is his habit to close letters with greetings in his own handwriting, so that in future they shall know authentic letters from mere forgeries (3:17, 2:2). This would seem more appropriate early in a correspondence than later. 'Do you not remember that when I was still with you I told you this' again sounds like a hint that they have forgotten very soon. The most one can fairly conclude is that what slight clues there are in the shorter letter to the time of its writing point to an earlier rather than a later date. If this is true, 3:1–2 probably looks back to the recent flight from Beroea.

There are, moreover, certain questions about the shorter letter which are difficult to resolve. The appeal in 2:5 and 3:10 is to what Paul said when at Thessalonica, not to anything he had previously written on the same theme in a longer missive. The longer letter seems entirely ignored in the shorter one. There is one clear reference to some previous correspondence, not relating to any point raised in the longer letter; we know that Paul wrote more than was preserved. ('Every letter of mine', 3:17, cannot refer to the longer epistle, which has no such signature.)

A larger question concerns *why* Paul wrote the shorter letter at all, if the church already possessed his longer treatment of the Advent theme. 'You have no need to have anything written to you' (1 Thessalonians 5:1) seems over-optimistic if the church needed *two* letters to get things clear. It is puzzling to see what *2 Thessalonians* clarifies 'concerning the coming of the Lord Jesus Christ', that *1 Thessalonians* had not already sufficiently explained, or that could not have been said there.

To this day, the shorter letter remains more puzzling than the longer! No new situation, or question, seems to call for *2 Thessalonians*, unless it be news of some believers living in idleness (3:11). But that topic comes too late in the shorter letter to be its main purpose.

Some scholars hold that the shorter letter, with its programme of events preparatory to Christ's advent, actually contradicts the longer letter, which teaches a sudden arrival of Christ, with cry, call, and trumpet, and 'like a thief in the night'.

Some think, too, that the comforting hope of Christ's coming, in the longer letter, is very different from the vindictive, Jewish-apocalyptic tone of the shorter letter, which expects Christ to slay with a breath and destroy by his appearing. They conclude that Paul could not have written *both* letters.

The longer letter is generally accepted as Paul's; its style, its harmony with the *Acts* story, and such echoes in early literature as one could expect of a letter so brief and so limited in theme, support this view. (If 1 Thessalonians 2:16, declaring that God's wrath has come upon the Jews at last, refers to the fall of Jerusalem in AD 70, then these words, at least, could not be by Paul. But the words could refer to the anti-Jewish riots in Corinth, where Paul is writing, Acts 18:16–17; or to the many troubles afflicting Palestine in the years leading up to AD 70.)

If *1 Thessalonians* is by Paul, it is concluded that the totally unnecessary shorter letter, with its contradictions, and a style 'at once like and unlike Paul's' is the work of a Christian, and perhaps well-meaning, imitator, using Paul's name.

This suggestion cannot be cursorily dismissed: it did happen. But the evidence, here, is hardly sufficient. A 'sudden' advent does not preclude preparation, unless 'sudden' means 'immediate'; while Paul could certainly use picturesque 'Jewish' language to describe divine judgement, especially when quoting a favourite Old Testament prophet (Isaiah 11:4, Romans 2:5–11, 1 Corinthians 3:13–15). The reference to Roman judicial authority holding lawlessness in check (if that is what 2 Thessalonians 2:6–7 means) is entirely Pauline (Romans 13:1–4).

That citations from the shorter letter are few and late is hardly surprising, from the nature of its contents. While an imitation, or forgery, which warns the readers against forgeries (2:2) implies a cynicism hardly compatible with any innocent Christian intention.

On the whole there seems insufficient reason for rejecting *2 Thessalonians*, and most (though not all) of the difficulties are resolved if we accept the time-clues already noted and conclude that *2 Thessalonians* is the earlier letter, and *1 Thessalonians* was written later to clarify remaining doubts.

The traditional order and numbering, of course, reflect only the ancient collectors' placing of the longer letter first, as more important. On this assumption, 1 Thessalonians 5:1 apparently means that it ought not to be necessary to write on behaviour before the advent, when the readers already had 2 Thessalonians 3:6–15.

Tentative Reconstruction

It appears that when Timothy, journeying from Macedonia at Paul's request, rejoined Paul at Athens, he reported continuing persecution over the region, and that some Thessalonian Christians were excited and confused about the promise of Christ's return. They were neglecting their daily work and ordinary responsibilities to look for Christ's appearing. Paul says that he sent Timothy back to establish the Thessalonians in their faith and to exhort them not to be moved by their afflictions (1 Thessalonians 3:1–5). This is precisely the message of 2 *Thessalonians*.

Giving thanks for the young church's spiritual progress, Paul says he boasts to others of its steadfastness in continuing persecution. He declares that this staunchness is itself evidence of God's having judged the members worthy to suffer for the kingdom. The same divine judgement will, when Christ returns, bring dire affliction on their persecutors, and relief to themselves. Paul prays that God will make them worthy of such a vocation and fulfil his purpose in them.

As to this coming of Christ, the Thessalonians should not be shaken, either by 'prophets' or by a letter purporting to be from Paul, to the effect that the Day of the Lord has already come (perhaps so interpreting their persecution). Widespread anarchy will come first, and the blasphemous 'anti-God' appear; the coming of such an 'anti-Christ' was a prominent part of early Christian prophecy (see 1 John 2:18, 4:3, Revelation 13). Meanwhile he is restrained (by Rome's power and law?), but he will eventually be revealed, with marvellous signs to deceive the unbelieving, and be ultimately destroyed at the coming of Christ.

So the Thessalonians should not lose faith; nothing is happening contrary to the teaching they had received; God's programme must be fulfilled. Meanwhile, Paul's thanksgiving for them, his assurances and good wishes, were all calculated to lift up their hearts. By asking for their prayers in return, in view of those who oppose himself, Paul hints that the readers do not suffer alone. He then repeats his assurance of God's faithfulness, and his own confidence, and closes the main message with a moving prayer that in their suffering their hearts may be directed to the *love* of God and the *steadfastness* of Christ.

The closing paragraph turns to Timothy's news of their idleness, depending on others earning for them, while they awaited Christ. Not so had they been taught. Paul repeats the command for converts to work quietly at their own livelihood. Those who refuse should be warned, and shunned. He wishes for all, in their suffering, the gift of peace, and the presence of the Lord of peace.

Having delivered this letter, and himself encouraged the Thessalonians for a while, Timothy returned again to Paul, by this time at Corinth (Acts 18:5). He brought further news, that persecution had subsided (1 Thessalonians 2: 14), and the Thessalonians had fulfilled all the rich promise of their beginning. He brought also some questions from the church, requiring the reply of *1 Thessalonians*. For three chapters Paul revelled in memories of those early days, mingling with warm compliments his own regrets at long absence. An appropriate prayer closes this section — that God will bring apostle and church together, and crown the beginning with continual progress.

Paul then adds an exhortation, on his own initiative before turning to the church's questions, concerning sexual morality and the sacredness of marriage. Everything we know of Corinth, where Paul was writing, makes it probable that the scenes he witnessed there prompted this plea for holiness in the church at Thessalonica. He then turns to questions, indicated by an expression, 'Concerning the...' ('Now as to...'), familiar in ancient literature and frequent in *1 Corinthians*, occurring here at 4.9,13, 5:1.

'Concerning brotherly love...' may well indicate a question evoked by what Paul had said in the shorter letter about 'keeping away from any brother who is living in idleness'. Was that loving? Should Christian shun brother Christian in a hostile world? Deliberately echoing what he had earlier written (2 Thessalonians 3:6–15, compare 12 with the later comment, 1 Thessalonians 4:11), Paul assures them that he knows of their great mutual love; he meant to ask only that it shall increase, alongside quiet attention to daily duties, self-supporting work. Love must not descend to sentiment, condoning irresponsible idleness.

'Concerning those who are asleep...' introduces a question raised by Paul's programme of events before Christ's advent. The Thessalonians had turned from idols 'to wait for God's Son from heaven', but already some believers had died, and by Paul's account others must do so before the Day of the Lord. Will they, then, miss the promised victory and glory? Paul replies that the dead will miss nothing; those alive at that time shall have no precedence. 'God will bring with him those who have fallen asleep' to share the triumph and be ever with the Lord. Let that be comfort to them all.

'Concerning the times and seasons...' suggests a question raised by what Paul had earlier written about the emergence of the man of sin, and the events that would follow. That suggests a gradual coming, or perhaps that Christ is present already, resisting evil. This is not the sudden glorious revelation and victory they had thought the gospel promised. Paul now completes the picture. Preparation tending towards denouement does not preclude a swift and glorious end, as travail (he says) leads to the climax of the birth, as plotting leads to the startling 'thief in the night'. The end will be sudden: yet believers should not be surprised, for they are sons of the Day. Immediately, the pastor replaces the prophet, to draw lessons of vigilance, soberness, well-armed alertness, as the best preparation for the advent. Paul then repeats his exhortations about obedience, respect for their leaders, mutual upbuilding and encouragement, with well-doing, joy, prayer, thankfulness, and freedom for the Spirit's ministry among them. Request for prayer, and that the letter be read to all, closes the second epistle to the Thessalonians (that is, 1 Thessalonians).

Meaning for Today

The purpose of both Thessalonian epistles is to encourage, in persecution, in bereavement, and in perplexity. Faced with persecution, Paul's encouragement lies in recalling that it had always been expected, in declaring that the Thessalonians' steadfastness is inspiring all the churches of Greece, and in promising that the persecutors themselves shall not escape judgement. It is easy for spectators at a safe distance to condemn the wish for justice; only those who have suffered such oppression, have seen homes destroyed, families massacred, innocent people tortured, can rightly assess the wish, or the language used.

In essence, Paul is promising final vindication of the gospel, of the believers now suffering, and of the Christ they worship and wait for. In a world where at any time, in almost any place, political, racial, or religious fanaticism may again bring bloodshed, torture and death to innocent lives, a more realistic and tough-minded Christian faith may become necessary to stiffen resistance and breed heroism. The certainty of God's judgement, that right will triumph, truth will endure, and Christ will reign, are indispensable to Christian survival.

The comfort which Paul offers in bereavement concentrates upon the oneness in Christ, and in ultimate reward, of the one church of Christ, whole and undivided, past and present, militant and triumphant. That the bonds of love and fellowship survive death is the very heart of the Christian hope; to be for ever with the Lord is its crown. Rarely, if ever, has Christian faith in immortality been more movingly expressed. Paul's six verses have brought strong comfort and hope to millions of hearts at Christian funeral services ever since, and will continue to do so as long as Christianity endures.

Modern Christians find Paul's third Thessalonian theme embarrassing. The hope of Christ's return thrilled the apostolic age, sang in the ancient *Te Deum*, proclaimed Christian optimism in the Creeds, in every succeeding age. 'Adventism' has persisted in the church, often muted, although the New

Testament itself bears witness to the disappointment which perplexed the early church. John stressed that Christ is present already, as the Spirit; *2 Peter* urged that with God a thousand years are but one day; Matthew emphasized that Jesus warned 'the End is not yet'.

Part of the modern difficulty is the failure of devout imagination to provide acceptable pictures of such an event; while so much of the ancient language (like Paul's own) is more reminiscent of the messianic hope that Jesus rejected, and of the triumphalism that persecution breeds, than of Christ's own values. The advent hope has in consequence become vague and elusive, a theological concept rather than a vital inspiration. And the Thessalonian letters, on this theme, are largely neglected.

Yet Christians must believe that God's purposes will not be finally defeated; that those purposes centre in Christ as Lord, and the future therefore belongs to him; and that the final act of divine redemption, like the first, will spring from God's intervention, and not from human wisdom, virtue, or effort. The Christian's hope for mankind is not in mankind, nor in the church, but in the sure promises of God that the end will be Christ's, and will therefore be good.

This is what Paul insists upon, in contemporary terms for which we may have to find substitutes. Then, again like a good pastor, Paul draws from the hope not detailed prophecies but lessons for daily living and incentives for courageous endurance. As Christianity will never be able to do without a future dimension, so these epistles will always have something to say to Christian hearts about the coming reign of Christ.

Suggestions for Group Discussion

1 Despite the Creed, *Te Deum*, and Advent season, the idea of Christ's second coming plays little part in modern Christianity. Why is this? Is anything important lost by it?

2 Does modern Christianity have a future dimension? Let the group formulate a statement of how they, as Christians, see the future developing, and the age ending.

3 1 Thessalonians 4:13–18 is used in many Christian funerals: does the group think it suitable? Let the group suggest other passages of scripture which it would wish to see so used, especially any which have been a help in bereavement.

4 To 2 Thessalonians 3:6–13 add Ephesians 4:28, and outline the Christian doctrine of work. Note carefully that both passages assume that work is *available*.

CHAPTER 7

Protracted Correspondence with Corinth

Preparatory Reading: Acts 18:1–28, 20:2,3, 1 Corinthians 1:1–2:5, 4:14–5:8, 6:9–11, 12:1–11, 2 Corinthians 1:23–2:17

Corinth was no place for young Christians. Like many seaports, where races and cultures mingle, ideals fade, and moral codes decline, mid-Mediterranean Corinth had an evil reputation, long-standing and well deserved. The very name was a by-word for vice and corruption of all kinds; to call someone's lifestyle 'Corinthian' was actionable slander in Greek courts. To list only those features reflected in Paul's letters: rich vineyards behind the city kept the quayside bars overflowing with potent wine; east-west trade provided immense wealth to nourish luxury and many casinos; temples abounded, to Apollo, Isis, Serapis, Demeter, Helios, all offering 'miracles' and various forms of ecstasy and divine possession, speaking with tongues, oracle-prophecies; the temple to Aesculapius made Corinth a centre of 'faith-healing', and that to Aphrodite provided innumerable sacred prostitutes, male and female.

Situated on the southern edge of declining Greece, Corinth shared the Greek love of argument and talk without the Greek intellect and love of truth; 'Corinthian words' stigmatized mere pretension to philosophy. A feminist movement aped men's hair, dress and manners, and the kind of public discussion hitherto exclusively masculine (recall woman's prominence at Philippi, Thessalonica and Athens, Acts 16:13–14, 17:4, 34). The unscrupulous merchant-trader, the libertine playboy, the athlete idolizing physical strength (Corinth hosted Games second only to the Olympics), and the broken dregs of humanity, were the acknowledged Corinthian 'types'.

Paul at Corinth

When, therefore, Paul came to Corinth from Athens, he plunged from the height of Greek culture to its depths, to confront paganism at its worst with the challenge of the gospel. Plainly, Corinth was another strategic centre, both geographically and spiritually, as Paul's two years' stay suggests (about AD 50–52); to succeed here would be to *prove* the gospel.

Corinth also involved risks, violent reactions, short-lived 'conversions', elementary problems of manners and morals, intense emotionalism, a longing to imitate the ecstasies and supernatural signs of the pagan shrines — together with undoubted miracles of divine grace. It is not surprising that the Corinthian church should be the problem-church of the New Testament: the wonder is that a church existed there at all.

Paul says he began in Corinth in fear, and with the determination to preach nothing but Christ, and him crucified. He may not have planned to stay long, intending to return to Thessalonica, but a night-vision laid Corinth upon his heart, bidding him remain.

Provoked by Paul's nearness (next door to the synagogue!) and by his success, Jews accused Paul before the proconsul Gallio (brother to Seneca, a Roman senator). Gallio's contemptuous dismissal of the charge as mere inter-Jewish rivalry established Christianity's freedom in the city, and led to a mob's attack upon the Jews.

Later when Paul revisited Corinth he was very ill received (2 Corinthians 2:1). About AD 56–57 he came again for three months (Acts 20:2–3), when again he was in danger from Jewish antagonism. Timothy and Silas shared Paul's first visit, and Timothy came also later, possibly delivering *1 Corinthians* (1 Corinthians 4:17 NIV); Titus also visited Corinth, perhaps twice (2 Corinthians 7:6–7,13, 8:6,16–17).

Whether Peter himself visited Corinth is uncertain; a partisan group emerged using his name, although nothing is said about controversy at Corinth over Jewish law, food taboos, circumcision or table-fellowship.

In subsequent letters sent to Corinth it is possible to find traces of attitudes and ideas, about wisdom, knowledge, marriage, the unimportance of the body as to sexual behaviour, resurrection and the like, which developed into the later 'gnosticism'; and also traces of theological emphases associated with a later group called 'Samaritans'. There is no evidence that such teaching troubled Corinth in Paul's time.

About 40 years after Paul's visits, Clement of Rome wrote to the church urging it to remember how Paul had exhorted it to unity! (Clement is the first of numerous early Christian writers who show no doubt that *1 and 2 Corinthians* are by Paul).

The Correspondence Begins

When Paul returned from Palestine to Ephesus (about AD 52–53), he learned that all was not well at Corinth, just across the Aegean, and he wrote urging that the church separate from 'immoral men' (1 Corinthians 5:9). This first letter to Corinth is lost; Paul refers to it because he is again urging a

Passover cleansing-out of old leaven, and because the Corinthians seem to have misunderstood.

'Separation' from paganism was necessary to Christians, as to strict Jews, to maintain character and witness; but Paul concedes that *total* separation is impracticable: he had meant withdrawal of fellowship from any claiming to be Christian who behaved immorally. Though lost, such a letter nevertheless affords a vivid glimpse into the practical problems facing a church in such a city.

Remembering the casual way in which Paul's letters were at first preserved, and the probability that notes were sometimes copied together on single papyri, we look with interest at a strange paragraph, obviously out of place at 2 Corinthians 6:14–7:1. This has no connection with what precedes or follows; the context reads much more smoothly without it, and its content is precisely what Paul refers to as the letter which Corinth misunderstood — not surprisingly, if Paul said 'be not mismated with unbelievers' when he meant 'with professing believers whose conduct shows them to be unbelievers', as he later explains. Did the church after all keep just a fragment of the 'lost' letter, and copy it where it did not belong?

While still at Ephesus, Paul received further disturbing news, carried by Stephanas, his first convert at Corinth and now a leader there, by Fortunatus, and Achaicus, who are apparently of 'Chloe's (business) people' (1 Corinthians 1:11, 16:15–17). These bring also a series of six or seven questions from the church (1 Corinthians 7:1) indicated (as in *1 Thessalonians*) by 'Concerning...', 'Now as to...'. Paul's response is one of the most important letters he ever wrote, our *1 Corinthians*, that is, the first to be preserved.

'1 Corinthians'

The address, 'to *saints* in *Corinth*', is a compliment; the thanksgiving is full of admiration and confidence, whatever Corinth's temporary problems.

• *News of Partisanship (1:10–4:21):* Paul rebukes divisions, naming his informants; he repudiates any 'Paul party' — Christ alone is Lord. What seems a digression disparaging worldly wisdom is, in fact, Paul's comment on the contrast being drawn between himself ('a poor speaker') and the eloquent Apollos (2 Corinthians 10:10, 1 Corinthians 4:6). Paul had renounced wisdom; how could the Corinthians, with their fleshly standards and nursery squabbling, have understood a more academic approach? Human leaders are only servants of the same God, who alone gives the harvest. One lays foundation, others build — at their own responsibility. Why compare teachers, when all have something to contribute? 'All are yours.' Paul submits only to God's judgement. The

Corinthians seem to think themselves rich, while apostles are poor! Relenting, he reminds his beloved children that, at any rate, he alone is their father through the gospel, and promises a visit.

- *News of Immorality (5, 6):* Details are lacking, but *apparently* incest passes unchecked. Paul requires the church to exclude the evil-doer. Explaining his earlier plea for separation, he mentions that he cannot judge outsiders; that leads to a digression on the Corinthians' readiness to take fellow Christians before pagan judges — which Paul rebukes. Resuming: the immoral have no place in God's Kingdom, as they should know, having been once cleansed. 'All things are lawful', perhaps, as some claim: but not all are expedient; some things enslave, some defile the body which Christ redeemed, which is his, and meant for resurrection, the temple of the *holy* Spirit.

- *Question: Concerning Marriage (7):* perhaps concerning celibacy, a topical issue. Paul says marriage is preferable to uncontrolled passion, and should be maintained. Jesus forbade divorce, though separation (without re-marriage to another) may be necessary where only one partner is converted, and the other demands freedom. The Christian should maintain the marriage if possible. In general, it is better to remain as converted-Jewish, slave (though not in heart), married, or single. In view of present troubles, and the nearness of the End, better remain free of anxieties, devoted to the Lord, but those who do marry do not sin. If any father (or lover) feels he is depriving his daughter (or betrothed) — let each decide what is best. A widow may marry again, to a Christian, but Paul thinks she would be *happier* not to.

- *Question: Concerning Idolatry (8–10):* Should Christians eat meat from idol-sacrifices (the usual source)? Paul quotes phrases from the church's discussions, warning against pride of knowledge. He concedes that idols are nothing, but some do not feel so. Let not your freedom injure them. He himself (for example) is free, as an apostle, to 'live off the gospel', as others do, as the scriptures allow; but he forgoes such freedom to avoid offence — and all other freedoms too, to serve the gospel. He recalls the solemn warning from ancient Israel's idolatry, to urge the Corinthians to avoid contact with it, lest they compromise with demons. To eat idol-meat privately does no harm, but if others make an issue of it, abstain.

- *Question: Concerning Worship (11:2–34):* The closing phrase suggests questions had been asked. Paul takes up one, concerning decorum in view of feminist freedom claimed at Corinth. Paul reiterates traditional Jewish ideas, while admitting that 'in the Lord' things are different! He assumes that women prophesy and pray in public, requiring only that they dress modestly when doing so. He dismisses the matter, to deal with a more serious want of decorum, which the church did *not* ask about! — disorder and drunkenness at the Lord's Table. He recounts the solemn institution of the Supper, and warns of God's judgement upon any irreverence, selfishness, or lack of perception of the Supper's meaning.

- *Question: Concerning Gifts of the Spirit (12–14):* All Christian gifts are at the disposal of the same Spirit; no one member of Christ's body can dispense with another, nor boast of his gift against another's. More excellent than all gifts is love, without which no gift is worth anything at all. Superior among all the gifts is prophecy (preaching). The 'tongues' prized so highly at Corinth because offered at heathen shrines, in practice edify no one, and to incoming strangers appear as madness. All gifts are to be exercised in orderly and considerate fashion. Women should not interrupt services with their questions, but ask their husbands at home for instruction. Obedience and order are essential to corporate worship.
- *News, or Question: Concerning the Resurrection (15):* Because some were questioning, not the immortality of the soul, as many Greeks held, but the resurrection of the body, which Jews and Christians taught as necessary to a whole personality, Paul rehearses the evidence of Christ's resurrection, as essential to the gospel. He expounds the Christian hope, and God's purpose for the End. But materialist views of the body are foolish; there are many kinds of 'body', and the resurrected body will be such as is adapted to immortal life. All will be changed, death will be conquered. So we should be steadfast in the work of God, for no labour will be in vain.
- *Question: Concerning Alms for Judea (16:1–11):* Paul suggests preparations, outlines his own plans, requests a welcome for Timothy, the letter-bearer.
- *Question: Concerning Apollos (16:12):* Apparently the church asked that Apollos return to Corinth; Paul claims the supposed rival as 'brother', and has urged him to return, but Apollos must decide for himself, and says 'Not now' (note Titus 3:13).
- *Closing instructions, greetings, and grace (16:13–24).*

(The suggestion has been made that Paul expected the reading of this letter in church assembly to be followed immediately by celebration of the Eucharist. 'Greet one another with a holy kiss' would begin the sacrament with the kiss of peace. 'If anyone love not the Lord Jesus let him be anathema' would formally exclude unbelievers from the service. 'Marana tha' — Aramaic for 'Come, Lord' — invokes the presence of Christ, and possibly his final advent, at his own table. A fascinating interpretation!)

Another 'Lost' Letter

Sending *1 Corinthians* had two serious consequences. The church was displeased, for Paul visited Corinth and experienced so hostile a reception that he hastily retreated. This visit, not mentioned by Luke, is clearly implied in 2 Corinthians 13:1–2 'my second visit', 12:14, 2:1 a 'painful visit'. It is evident that he 'warned those who sinned' with some vigour, and the proud Corinthians resented it.

Back in Ephesus (apparently) and deeply hurt, but unwilling to abandon his rebellious converts, Paul tried a third letter. This also was stern, written 'out of much affliction and anguish of heart, with many tears, not to cause pain' but to demonstrate his anxious pastoral care, and that he might test their obedience (2 Corinthians 2:4,9). This is the letter that at one point Paul regretted writing, and which indeed grieved the church deeply (2 Corinthians 7:8). And Paul feared its outcome. Titus had taken the letter, and when Paul visited Troas to preach and did not find Titus returned and awaiting him, his mind 'could not rest', he could not preach, but pressed on through Macedonia to meet Titus.

Knowing (from *Galatians*) how strongly Paul could write when someone undermined his work and troubled his converts, we would give much to have this third letter to Corinth. But apparently it was not preserved. Or not all? For here another intriguing possibility opens up. As we shall see, Titus brought excellent news from Corinth, and a gracious, warm-hearted, grateful letter of reconciliation sealed the sorry story. All was well again, confidence was restored; this is emphasized in 2 Corinthians 1–7/9. But quite suddenly, in 2 Corinthians 10–13, Paul's tone changes completely. These are by far the sharpest chapters we have from Paul's pen, full of invective, argument, sarcasm, self-justification, boasting (admitted to be folly), solemn warning, and at the end a demand that the readers examine themselves, whether they are still Christians, and the call to 'Mend your ways'.

Appealing by the meekness and gentleness of Christ, Paul repeats some of the epithets hurled against himself, and warns of punishment for disobedience. He affirms his authority, again quotes the readers' abuse, rejects any comparison with others, and reminds that he first brought the gospel to Corinth.

He speaks of fears and jealousy over them, and ironically compares with their treatment of himself their great readiness to welcome his detractors, 'these superlative apostles!' He defends his independence when among them, calls the 'false apostles' disguised servants of Satan, boasts again, foolishly — but they tolerate fools! — and recounts his long service of Christ. He then explains his present physical weakness and pain as God's way of keeping him humble, after so great revelations and privileges.

Again Paul calls his boasting 'folly', and apologizes for not burdening them. More gently, he urges his former care of them, and fears that when he next comes he may still find them angry, quarrelling, selfish, disorderly, impenitent.

Further warning, and the challenge to re-examine their position, lead to hopes and prayers for amendment; and the wish that he may not again have to use authority severely. The four chapters end with brief greeting and grace.

The incoherence, repetition, and sudden changes of mood, as much as the language and forthrightness, eloquently reveal the strong feeling behind the passage; Paul is hurt, angry, accusing, and regretful in turn, with no word to placate, and certainly no hint of reconciliation, only of submission.

What can possibly be made of this? There is no sufficient ground to question that Paul wrote these chapters; but why a letter of joyous thanksgiving for reconciliation, full of affirmations of mutual confidence, should end in this way defeats explanation. Various hypotheses have been offered: Paul received another letter, or further bad news, from Corinth — but that would require a new letter, not a totally contradictory postscript. Paul was subject to constant interruption, or 'a sleepless night' — hardly Christian excuses for *sending* such a missive! Paul now addresses the stubborn minority in the church — then why does he not say so? Nothing in the earlier chapters suggests that he was there apeaking to only part of the membership; nor would the report of Titus have overjoyed Paul had it told of continued sharp division.

As *2 Corinthians* now stands in the New Testament, Paul suddenly reverts to the earlier quarrel, reopens the charges and counter-charges, takes back all the warm thanksgiving, forgiveness, and confidence of 1–7, and prolongs the ill-feeling with new bitter words. All without explanation — though it may be questioned if any explanation would make such tactics Christian!

The suggestion springs to mind, the only one which even approaches satisfaction, that 2 Corinthians 10–13 is, in fact, part of that stern sorrowful letter which Paul regretted writing, but which brought the Corinthians through grief to a better mind. The possibility is attractive, even persuasive. Some confirmation could be found in the way that certain verses in 2 Corinthians 1–7/9 would then look *back* to verses in 10–13—2:9, on testing their obedience, would allude to 10:6, which mentions punishing disobedience; 1:23 — Paul not visiting in order to spare them — would echo 13:2 'If I come I will not spare'; 2:3 — 'I wrote as I did so that when I came I might not be pained' — would recall 13:10 'I write this in order that when I come I might not have to be severe'; 5:12; 'We are not commending ourselves to you *again*' would have greater meaning because he and they remembered how he had done so in 11:21–33, 12:11–12.

The copying of two letters on to a single papyrus is no difficulty, but what happened to the original ending of the reconciling letter and the opening of the severe letter is still unexplained. The most that can honestly be claimed is that this suggestion is the best hypothesis available, while the alternative, that Paul suddenly took back all the fine things he had written, is quite unacceptable.

'2 Corinthians'

Whatever we decide about 2 Corinthians 10–13, a severe letter was sent, did its work, and sent Titus back to Paul with news which thrilled his heart. The story of the reconciliation, and Paul's reflections upon it, make up '2 Corinthians', Paul's *fourth* letter to Corinth, written from Macedonia.

- *Address, Greeting, Thanksgiving (1:1–11):* The thanksgiving is especially full and heartfelt because the 'comfort' given by the news from Corinth arrived after great affliction suffered in Ephesus; not only the Corinthians have been in trouble.
- *Explanations, Reassurances (1:12–2:17):* Paul explains why he had not visited Corinth again, to spare them; but regretted writing so sternly. Meeting Titus, he had learned that God had again led them all in the (Roman) 'Triumph' of Jesus (2:14–16). From 2:5–10 we learn that one individual caused most trouble, probably not the immoral man of 1 Corinthians 5:1–5. Answering the criticism that he changed his mind about his plans, Paul side-glances at Christ as the utterly dependable 'Yes' of God to all his promises of good.
- *The Christian Ministry (3:1–6:13):* Apparently a digression, but since the relation of apostle to church has been at the heart of the quarrel, it is appropriate to the moment of healing to set the relationship right, especially as a ministry of reconciliation (see 4:5,15, 5:12,18–20). As to 'recommendations', Paul says that the transformed Corinthians are the best recommendations he could desire. But all has come from God, who has granted a ministry of the Spirit, of freedom, of clear vision of God, greater than anything even Moses exercised. Paul analyzes the motives and resources that sustain him (in spite of Ephesus and Corinth) — the memory of God's mercy, the daily renewal of Christ's life within, the hope of immortality, the constraint of Christ's love, the privilege of an ambassador proclaiming reconciliation. He appeals, therefore, for renewed acceptance and affection.
- *Explanations, Reassurances Resumed (7:2–16):* (6:14–7:1 a misplaced paragraph — see above). Paul's appeal for acceptance merges into renewed expressions of comfort, confidence, and joy, that all strife is past.
- *Appeals for Contributions (8, 9):* The collection 'for relief of the saints' in

Judea should now proceed. Paul holds up the example of Macedonia's generosity, that Titus might evoke similar response at Corinth; Paul speaks of Christ's generosity, also. What was begun a year ago, before the quarrel, should now be completed; Paul's arrangements are explained (see chapter 8). Paul then urges his boasting to Macedonia about Corinth's readiness and generosity, as a reason for Corinth's fulfilling its promise. Scriptural reasons are added, and the promise of rewarding blessing, through the grateful prayers of those who will receive, and through the 'inexpressible' gift of God (see chapter 9).

Some have felt that an appeal for money would be out of place immediately after strife. Others, with perhaps more pastoral experience, perceive that to resume exactly where things went wrong, and ask a favour, is often the best way to leave a quarrel behind. In that light, chapter 8 seems altogether appropriate here. Chapter 9, however, does seem unnecessary here. We need care, though; once the suggestion that separate notes might be copied together has been found helpful anywhere, it is tempting to find it everywhere. Each offered example must be examined on its merits.

But the new start at 9:1, as though chapter 8 had not been written, especially beginning 'It is superfluous for me to write to you about the offering for the saints...', is exceedingly odd. So is the fact that in 9:5 'the brethren' who are to stimulate their giving are already sent ahead, whereas in 8:17 Titus is then being sent for the same purpose. Repeated reference to Macedonia, and new arguments for generosity, add to the suspicion that chapter 9 might well be an earlier, pre-quarrel note about the collection, now preserved at the end of the reconciling letter (1–8).

- *The Quarrel Resumed?* (*10–13*): Examined above.

Timeless Value

Considering its unhappy features, Paul's correspondence with Corinth came to possess extraordinary importance. Some part of the passage on the Lord's Supper finds a place in every form of the Eucharist, at almost every celebration, throughout the world.

Paul's discussion of the resurrection, too, brings comfort and victory into almost every Christian funeral. The hymn to love is one of the best known passages in all literature.

Paul's exposition of the place of the Spirit in Christian worship has reminded the church repeatedly that worship is no merely human experience. That it has provoked much fruitless debate is largely because modern Christians forget its original background, when Corinthian converts longed to emulate the spiritual 'wonders' and ecstasy which their pagan friends could boast. Paul steadily plays down the stranger manifestation of this fervour, in favour of prophecy, order, and, above all, love.

As for *2 Corinthians*, Paul's analysis of the nature, motives, aims and resources of the Christian ministry obviously has permanent value.

Both letters contribute much to our understanding of Paul himself. Nor could we forget, in these days, that the underlying problem in both letters has to do with Christian life and work in an 'inner city' atmosphere of secularism, vice, decay, violence, and racial stress. The ideals, the dangers, the resources, and the needed moral wisdom which such a situation demands are nowhere more thoroughly explored. If the form of each problem changes with the centuries, the essence of each, and of the Christian solution, remains the same. The gospel which saved and armed the Corinthians is still Christianity's only answer to the challenge of city life in an age fast returning to pre-Christian ways.

Suggestions for Group Discussion

1 With Paul's quarrel at Corinth in mind, a speaker recently called for more 'creative friction' in the church. Would the group agree that such friction is better than complacency, coldness, dullness, endless harmony?

2 Corinth represents the New Testament's 'inner city' with its innumerable social and moral problems: what particular emphases should mark the church's gospel in such a situation?

3 What does the group make of the advice Paul gives about meat that has been killed on idol-altars, in 1 Corinthians 8:1–13, 10:19–33. Is it consistent — or is Paul still thinking?

4 Suggest that the group chooses some Christian cause known to be in need of money, and drafts an appeal letter on the lines, and using the arguments, of 2 Corinthians 8 and 9.

CHAPTER 8

Confusion at Colossae

Preparatory Reading: Colossians

The Colossian church was a step-child of Paul. When, on his third missionary journey, he passed through 'the upper country' of Phrygia (in Asia Minor) to reach Ephesus, he by-passed Colossae, 100 miles east of Ephesus, and as far as we know never visited there (Acts 18:23, 19:1, Colossians 2:1). But Paul's powerful three-year mission in the beautiful capital ensured that 'all the residents of Asia heard the word of the Lord'. Among these were Philemon, Archippus, and Epaphras, all (almost certainly) of Colossae (Colossians 4:2). Although 'Epaphras' is a common shortening of 'Epaphroditus', the name occurs too often to identify Colossae's pastor with Philippi's representative.

For Epaphras carried his new-found faith back home and 'worked hard' to found a church there, and also at Laodicea and Hierapolis, 10 and 13 miles away respectively. The local road system brought streams of travellers to Colossae with news and new ideas from east and west. Two thousand Jewish families had settled there, forming an initial audience for the gospel. And a virile native paganism, making superstitious use of an underground river, a petrified waterfall, sulphur springs, a 'poison gas' chasm, and frequent earthquakes, kept religious feelings and fears alive. It was needy but receptive soil for Christianity, but also for distortions of it. Epaphras was a Gentile, and so mainly was the Colossian church; few Old Testament allusions occur in Paul's letter, and only passing references to the Jewish-Gentile controversy.

When problems arose, Epaphras visited Paul to seek advice, and report the progress of the work. Paul mentions that the report was good (1:4,7), and seems to go out of his way to commend Epaphras' authority and ministry. He is 'our beloved fellow-servant, a faithful minister of Christ on our behalf', from whom the Colossians had 'learned the grace of God *in truth*', a 'servant of Christ' who 'has worked hard' for the Colossians. It would appear that some opposition to their 'unofficial' pastor had arisen in the church.

Authorship

This account of the origin of Colossians has, however, been questioned, mainly because the style of the writing in places is somewhat laboured, unlike

Paul's; some 25 words occur which Paul does not use elsewhere. We recall again that Pauline authorship does not necessarily imply Paul's penmanship; but here, also, Paul is discussing some strange teaching, which requires exceptional language, and in several places the borrowing of the 'heretics'' terminology.

The discussion leads Paul to say more than hitherto about the pre-existence and pre-eminence of Christ, but not more than some earlier statements imply (Christ the power and wisdom of God, 1 Corinthians 1:24; 'one Lord, Jesus Christ, through whom are all things and through whom we exist' 1 Corinthians 8:6; 'he was rich... became poor... that you might be rich' 2 Corinthians 8:9). There are parallels equally mind-stretching, too, in Romans 8, Philippians 2. If it be true that the structure and tone of Colossians 1:15–20, and its grammatical detachment from its context, show it to be a quotation from a familiar hymn, then its lofty thought was already current in Christian worship.

The close connection of *Colossians* with *Philemon*, the most surely Pauline of all letters, supports the claim of the opening and closing verses that Paul was the author, and from second-century Latin translations onwards, the letter is regularly treated as Paul's. For long it was thought that the heresy here opposed belonged to the second century, too late for the apostle to comment upon. We now know that the elements which comprised that later 'gnosticism' had infected unorthodox Judaism much earlier. A Christian *essay* opposing gnosticism sometime in the second century, and published in Paul's name, would certainly be conceivable; but to invent the whole situation presupposed by *Colossians*, Epaphras' visit, greetings from Luke and others, the journey of Titus, the prayers, in order to give a pamphlet the appearance of truth, would betray a mind itself not far removed from heresy, after all. It is right to consider objections, but on the whole the conclusion must surely be that Paul dictated Colossians.

Where was Paul?

Paul's circumstances at the time are only partially clear. He is in prison, 'in fetters'; but where? Paul says he was 'in prisons oft' but Luke mentions imprisonment only at Philippi and Caesarea, with 'house arrest', apparently without fetters, in Rome.

Clearly Luke's account is incomplete; equally clearly, *Colossians* was not written during the one night at Philippi, or at Caesarea, where Paul is about to appeal to Caesar, involving a sea journey, long delay awaiting trial, and then, if freed, would mean a 1,000-mile journey back to Colossae. Yet in *Philemon*, which was sent with *Colossians*, Paul asks that a room be prepared for him! Moreover it is most improbable that Paul had with him at Caesarea all the friends mentioned in Colossians.

But Rome is no more probable as the place of origin of *Colossians* and *Philemon*. The same delay, uncertainty of the future, and long journey to Colossae, makes the request for a room inconsiderate. In any case, by the time Paul reached Rome he had long announced his resolve not to work again in the east, but to pioneer westwards (Romans 15:17–24). Luke certainly gives the impression that Paul was not fettered before trial at Rome (Acts 28:16, 30–31, with 22:29). Nor is it at all probable that the runaway Onesimus would make for Rome: distance, and travel-obstacles, would be insuperable for a slave, even with stolen money. Ephesus was the obvious hiding-place.

Paul's three years at Ephesus included 'many adversaries'; 'hunger, thirst, nakedness, buffeting, homelessness, reviling, persecution, defamation' ('to the present hour', written from Ephesus, 1 Corinthians 4:11–13); 'affliction... perplexity... persecution... being struck down...'; 'great toil' (implying no support); 'many tears, temptations, plotting by Jews'; 'fighting with beasts' (whether literally or metaphorically); 'afflictions... unbearably crushed, so that we despaired of life itself... felt we had received the sentence of death... so deadly a peril' (written from Macedonia, about Ephesus). Only the word 'prison' is missing; Luke *omits it all.*

It is a question whether a free Roman could be in such danger without formal arrest and imprisonment. But Paul's phrase 'in prisons often' (2 Corinthians 11:23, compare 6:5), written from either Ephesus or Macedonia, when as far as we know he had only been in prison at Philippi, leaves no doubt that Paul was imprisoned at Ephesus. (A gospel prologue written at Ephesus in mid-second-century asserts that he was.) The strongest probability is, therefore, that *Colossians* and *Philemon*, the flight of Onesimus, the visit of Epaphras (so much easier from Colossae to Ephesus than to Rome), and that request to prepare a room, all centred in the prison at Ephesus.

What was Wrong?

After a long and very tactful preamble, Paul reaches the real purpose of his letter at 2:6–7: 'As therefore you received Christ Jesus the Lord, so live in him, rooted and built up in him, and established in the faith just as you were taught... See to it that no one makes a prey of you by philosophy and empty deceit... not according to Christ'. The specific dangers Paul has in view are then described; fortunately, we do not need to understand every detail in order to appreciate Paul's very positive reply.

All three elements in Colossae's background seem to have contributed to the church's present confusion. Jewish emphasis fell upon sabbath-keeping, circumcision, the law, festivals, and the 'new moon' holy days. Tension between Jews and Gentiles is mentioned only incidentally (3:11, 4:11). Elements probably pagan included the worship of 'angels', the widespread fear of heavenly beings who ruled the earth and needed to be placated. This fear nourished astrology, because sun, moon, stars, and seasons were in some sense embodiments of the ruling demonic or divine power. Rigorous self-abasement and 'devotion' was apparently also demanded. Fear of Greek influence seems to prompt Paul's warning against 'philosophy' built upon plausible reasoning and man-made tradition. The reference to being 'puffed up' without reason by a sensuous mind and to taking one's stand upon visions (the translation here is very uncertain) recalls the ecstatic trances promised by certain eastern and Greek religious cults.

Reference to the prohibition of certain food and drink, associated with 'repression of the body', suggests the Greek dualism between matter and spirit, with resulting religious austerities; a few phrases like 'inheritance in light', 'dominion of darkness' have the same flavour. So do the many allusions to wisdom and understanding (nine times), knowledge (seven times), secret, or mystery (four times), and 'fullness, filled' (five significant times). For these are watchwords of that gnosticism which in its many forms was made up of intellectual speculation, superstition, magic, ascetic demands and obscene rites (depending on how its fundamental tenets were interpreted).

Salvation was by the knowledge of divine mysteries and morality did not matter. The material world and the spiritual were totally opposed — matter being considered intrinsically, incurably evil. So the body may be violently suppressed, to liberate the spirit; or it may be indulged as quite irrelevant to 'spiritual' salvation. God, being pure spirit, could not have created, loved, or saved, the material world; he is far off, totally transcendent. Nor could God have become man. Between God and everything material (including man) stretched an infinite graded chain of spirit-beings, each a little *less* spiritual, *more* material, than the one above him. This chain is 'the fullness' filling the chasm separating God from creation.

One hopes that no one Christian at Colossae tried to absorb all these disparate ideas! Judaism had already its magical fringe (Acts 13:6, 19:13–17), and Simon the Magician (Acts 8:9–13) came to be called the father of gnosticism. Traces of gnostic ideas have been found in *Galatians, 1 John* and *Revelation*. It is most probable that the rudimentary trends and speculations that became gnosticism were troubling the church at Colossae and deeply disturbing Epaphras.

Plainly these ideas seriously obscured the *unique* divinity of Christ, and the fundamental truth of salvation by faith alone. Ethically this religious theosophy was intellectualist, individualist, elitist, despising the ordinary Christian; *love, unity,* had no place in gnostic attitudes. That is the immediate reason why Paul emphasizes his commission to 'warn *every* man, teach *every* man in all wisdom, that he may present *every* man fully initiated in Christ'. In addition, the cultic rituals and observances, and austere prohibitions associated with gnostic sects could only divert attention from the Christian sacraments, prayer, true self-discipline, and mutual love.

Paul's Reply

Colossians flows smoothly, without discernible structure except as the argument shapes the outline. The thanksgiving at once makes clear why Paul writes to a church he did not found — he has 'heard' of their faith, love, hope (the familiar triad). They have already heard, as he well knows, the truth of the gospel, and it has borne its usual fruit among them, following the faithful teaching of Epaphras. Then follows the appropriate prayer, for knowledge, wisdom, understanding, but Paul asks knowledge of God's will (not of mysteries), and wisdom that is spiritual (not speculative). This will enable a life worthy, pleasing, fruitful, and growing — the practical emphasis of the pastor. He asks also strength for endurance, with deep gratitude for all that God has done through his Son.

Mention of God's Son kindles a lyrical paragraph (some think a quotation from a hymn) extolling the cosmic pre-eminence of Christ, the image of the invisible God, firstborn of creation, the one in whom, through whom, and for whom, all was made, and in whom all things hold together. For it is in Christ that all the fullness of God chose to dwell, and through Christ that God reconciled all things to himself by the cross. That leaves little room for gnostic fancies about filling any gap between God and man: God has filled it with Christ. Already pre-eminent over all spiritual beings (real or imagined), Christ became also, Paul will say, their head and ruler, and their conqueror (1:16, 2:10,15).

The hymn to Christ is suddenly personalized: 'and *you,* once estranged, hostile, he has reconciled', provided that they continue in the faith they received, along with the whole church, 'stable, steadfast, not shifting'. Of this gospel Paul was a servant, glad to suffer for Christ's church, glad to make God's word known to every sort of man.

Paul's aim, even for those he does not know, is that they may be encouraged, and enriched with all wisdom and knowledge — but '*in Christ*', so that no one may delude them with plausible talk about fanciful speculations, merely human traditions, so-called elemental spirits of the universe. What have all these empty deceits to offer *Christians*? In Christ the whole *fullness* of deity dwells, and Christians have come to *fullness* of life in him. *What more can they possibly want than fullness of life in Christ the fullness of God?*

Gentiles though they are, they have in Christian baptism all that Jewish circumcision meant, 'the putting away of the flesh'. They are made alive with Christ; their sins have been forgiven, all charges against them nailed to Christ's cross. There Christ disarmed and shamed the so-called principalities and powers; they are no longer to be feared. As for trivialities people make much of — foods, festivals, sabbaths — all are mere shadows of religion: Christ is the substance, the great reality.

So too with public self-abasement, angel worship, pretended visions: what need has the Christian of any of it? Since you died with Christ to the world, its spirit-beings, its religious regulations, its precepts and theories, are but a mere show of wisdom, fostering merely ritual piety, formal humility, austere self-torture — why do you still live as though these things mattered? They are of no practical use in subduing sensuality. It is far more effective to be raised with Christ, to set one's mind where Christ is, seated at God's right hand, your life hidden with Christ in God, awaiting glory. *What more can you want?*

At this point (3:5) Paul begins to draw out the practical consequences of being so filled with Christ, possibly following closely the order of topics touched upon in the elementary convert-education which Paul often echoes, along with other New Testament writers. As elsewhere, the expressions 'put off, or away' (the old life), 'put to death' (the old nature), 'put on' (the new nature, the garments and sash of the renewed soul), show the baptismal context of thought. Here the fullness of life in Christ is overflowing in individual character.

So it must overflow in shared worship, also, as with the greeting of peace, thanksgiving, the uttered word of Christ dwelling richly in all minds, the members teach and exhort one another with psalms, hymns and spiritual songs — all in the name of the Lord, Jesus. Again the fullness of Christ will overflow in Christian homes, wives taking due place, husbands showing love and gentleness, children obedient, so pleasing the Lord, fathers avoiding provocation of the children. So Christ–likeness spreads through the family circle.

Likewise in daily work, slaves will give generous service, as to Christ, and masters will treat slaves fairly and justly, as being answerable to the supreme master in heaven (three revolutionary ideas, destined to end slavery in time).

Being filled with Christ will show yet further in Christian service, as Christians work and pray together, with all who bear the gospel. And in the daily testimony each bears towards outsiders, using every opportunity, with grace, intelligence, and wit (which Athenians called 'salt'), knowing how to present the truth appropriately to all types of people. With the fullness of God dwelling in Christ, and the fullness of Christ dwelling in each believer, overflowing to the circumference of each life — what more can any Christian possibly want, or know, or do?

Paul commends his messengers, includes greeting (from Mark, and another Jesus, and others), asks that Colossae and Laodicea exchange letters, and sends a bracing word to Archippus (apparently son of Philemon and Apphia, newly commissioned to ministry) to 'fill full his ministry'. After a reminder in his own handwriting of his present fetters, Paul closes with a grace. A brief letter, packed with ideas which Epaphras — returning with the apostle's fullest support — will be able to elaborate and apply. Since Christianity survived in the district for at least 300 years, we may assume Paul's letter was successful.

Permanent Value

In few biblical passages is the close relation of a true theology with a rich spiritual experience so plainly illustrated. A meagre view of Jesus always produces a shallow Christian life. Paul's deep, probing, breath-taking reach of thought about Christ in this letter — the cosmic Christ, agent in creation, the unity of the world, pre-eminent in all things, unrivalled in the church, first-born from the dead, the great reality among all the shadows of religion, reconciling heaven and earth, filled with the fullness of God — all that thrilling vision of the unique Christ of God arose in reaction against speculations threatening to displace Christ in Christian hearts!

And with the vision came the realization of the measureless horizons of Christian life, as the fullness of Christ flows outwards through believers into church, home, and outside world. Such a view of Christian faith and life can never be outdated.

With the Colossians we learn, too, the futility of seeking some 'new religious experiences' outside of Christ. To chase every new cult, every fresh 'school' of religious thought, every new fashion of 'spirituality', is merely to confess that Christ does not satisfy us, does not fill our lives with the fullness of God. Which raises the question, Whose fault can that be? All the added rites, disciplines, 'exercises', and self-imposed denials, may be good in their way — but they might be 'shadows' which displace the reality. To grasp clearly the immensity of Christ, experience fully the plenitude of Christ, is to be carried beyond all substitutes and armed against all distractions. Paul still challenges the church and the Christian: You have a great Saviour; what more can you possibly need, or hope to find?

Suggestions for Group Discussion

1 Is the view of Christ expounded in Colossians 1:13–20 still our view of him, or have we so humanized Jesus, so brought him down to our level, so 'identified Christ in our neighbour', as to make Paul's view of Christ meaningless?

2 Paul's argument is that there is no need to seek any further 'experiences', visions, power, or blessing, than we already have in Christ. Would the group agree that every new cult, movement, 'ism', fashion in religion, exposes some inadequacy in the church's presentation of the gospel? (Examples: Salvation Army, 'charismatic' movement, Spiritualism, house-groups, etc.)

3 Let the group trace, list, and examine the seven references to gratitude in *Colossians*'s four short chapters; then note the causes for thanksgiving which Paul names, and consider *why* Paul is so emphasizing this master-motive of the Christian life.

CHAPTER 9

A Pastoral Circular

Preparatory Reading: Acts 19:1–41, 20:17–38, Ephesians 1–4

To illustrate Paul's tremendous impact upon the city of Ephesus, Luke tells us that 'a number who had practised sorcery brought their scrolls together and burned them publicly. When they calculated the value of the scrolls, the total came to fifty thousand days' wages' (NIV with margin).

It has often been remarked that this great sacrifice of books was more than compensated for by the six short but infinitely rich chapters with which Paul replaced them. For many people, *Ephesians* is Paul's masterpiece. Its exultation of spirit, its intensely packed thought, and its many memorable verses, can still leave the reader breathless. One may imagine that the secretary, trying to keep up with Paul's dictation, must often have been left behind. 'Paul at his best, the Ephesians at their most fortunate!'

Such tributes assume, of course, that Paul wrote this letter, and that he wrote it to the church at Ephesus. That seems obvious — but there are difficulties, which must be faced fairly. One is the epistle's astonishing likeness to *Colossians*, in mood, thought, language, and partly in theme. *Ephesians* proves to be essentially a meditation on Colossians 1:20–22: 'through Christ (the fullness of God was pleased) to reconcile to himself all things, whether on earth or in heaven, making peace by the blood of his cross'.

Again and again in *Ephesians* one comes upon echoes of *Colossians*: 'Dead in trespasses... made alive in Christ'; 'in him we have redemption... the forgiveness of sins'; 'he made known... the mystery'; 'the word of truth, the gospel'.

Sometimes the ideas rhyme though the expression varies: 'Christ, head over all things for the church... his body' (*Colossians*: 'head of the body, the church... in all things pre-eminent'); Christ 'sitting in heavenly places' (*Colossians*: 'Christ sitteth at the right hand of God'); 'Put off your old nature... corrupt through deceitful lusts' (*Colossians*: 'You have put off the old nature with its practices'); 'addressing one another in psalms and hymns and spiritual songs, singing...' (*Colossians*: 'teach and admonish one another... as you sing psalms and hymns and spiritual songs...').

Thirty-nine such echoes of one short epistle in the other have been found, a few words ('mystery', 'stewardship', 'reconciling') being somewhat differently applied. The commendation of Tychicus in *Ephesians* differs from that in *Colossians* by only two Greek words out of 32. Would *Paul* ever so repeat himself?

A second difficulty concerns the style of writing in *Ephesians*. Some sentences are very long, and involved, synonyms are multiplied (four different words for power, for example), while some 40 Greek words occur which Paul uses nowhere else ('the heavenlies', 'godless', '*diabolos*' for Satan, are examples), though a number (like 'dart', 'firm-footing') are not likely to occur unless the same things are being said. For these reasons, the letter in Greek does not sound like Paul's. Some experts, after elaborate counting and comparison with *Romans, 1 Corinthians*, declare that linguistic analysis leaves the authorship of Ephesians an open question.

A third difficulty has been found in the apparently late date of the epistle. It is said that the letter presupposes a fully organized church ministry (4:11–12), not achieved until after Paul's time. All contention over Jewish-Gentile relationships seems now to have been left far behind (2:11–22). And a phrase like 'the mystery...has now been revealed to his *holy apostles* and prophets...' (3:4–5) seems to look backward to the apostolic age.

It may be replied that by the time of his Ephesus mission Paul had been organizing churches and arguing the Jewish question for nearly 20 years. While comparison with Colossians 1:26 ('the mystery... now made manifest to his *saints*' = 'holy ones') suggests that Paul may have intended 'saints, apostles, prophets' in *Ephesians*. Doubt remains, though not insolubly.

A Circular for Asia?

A fourth, and more serious, difficulty about Paul writing in this way to Ephesus is the total lack of local references. He had ministered there for three tumultuous years; many converts were made, many 'extraordinary miracles' had occurred, much had been suffered. The relation of *Ephesians* to *Colossians* shows that neither could have been written early in those years — not until Colossae and Laodicea had been founded. Yet there is not a single reminder, not one name of an Ephesian convert, helper, or fellow-sufferer, not a greeting or a thanksgiving, that betrays local knowledge. Indeed, the author says 'I have *heard* of your faith', 'assuming you have *heard* of the stewardship given to me', '*assuming* you have heard about Christ, and were taught in him...' (1:15, 3:2, 4:21).

It is noticeable, too, that Paul appeals for acceptance of his counsel on the grounds of his apostleship for Gentiles, and his imprisonment for Christ, not because of what he has previously done among his readers. These awkward facts cannot be evaded; either *Ephesians* was not by Paul, or it was not intended for Ephesus.

One other curious fact must be added to the puzzle. Several ancient copies of *Ephesians* still exist which do not bear any address at 1:1, among them copies from about AD 200 and from the fourth century. Six important early Christian writers reveal that they knew of such copies. Evidently, either these unaddressed copies arose because someone deleted the address to make the epistle a general message to the churches, or the epistle was from the first a general encyclical to a group of churches, and only gained its familiar name and the address later, when associated with Ephesus in the tradition of the church. Both Ignatius and Polycarp, in the early second century, and both writing from Smyrna, knew the epistle as Paul's, but some think Ignatius did not regard it as sent to Ephesus. Marcion, about AD 150, called the epistle 'To the Laodiceans', believing it to be Paul's, but knowing it to lack an address.

Reviewing the probabilities, it seems most likely that Paul himself used again ideas and phrases he had used in *Colossians*, varying them freely as he wished, for the benefit of a wider circle of readers. We know that many in Asia heard the word of God from his mission to Ephesus; others, like Epaphras, had carried their new faith homewards; and 'daughter-churches' of Ephesus eventually existed not only at Laodicea and Colossae, but at Hierapolis, Philadelphia, Sardis, Pergamum, Thyatira, Smyrna. Like Colossae, none of these had 'seen his face', but as churches arose in each place, he would have *heard* of their faith, and they of him (as *Ephesians* says).

This would explain the absence of names and reminiscences connected with his work in Ephesus; and the likeness-with-difference when compared with *Colossians* — a mere imitator would have copied more closely. It would suggest a reason for the early copies without an address.

Some have found several expressions of warm, yet not personal, feeling in the letter (1:15–16, 3:13–19, 4:1, 5:1, 6:21–22); this would be appropriate in a circular to daughter-churches. Further, it is possible to trace some ideas referred to in *Colossians* but more fully developed in *Ephesians*, detached from immediate, local needs; the idea of the church, for example; the relation of husband and wife; the wider significance of reconciliation.

Letters so similar almost imply simultaneous production, and the identical commendation of Tychicus in the two letters shows that *Ephesians* would be carried, with *Colossians*, by the same courier. (One ingenious guess would add that if the letter were passed from church to church, coming to Colossae last — see map — then *Ephesians* would reach Colossae as 'the epistle *from* Laodicea', so explaining Colossians 4:16. A little too clever to be true?)

A Magnificent Message
That these uncertainties do not affect our appreciation of the epistle's

meaning tends in itself to confirm that it is a circular, not closely involved with one church's problems. The thanksgiving is somewhat formal, as such a circular might well begin. Paul blesses God for all the enriching gifts of salvation, emphasizing especially the divine *purpose*, in words like 'chose us', 'destined', 'the purpose of his will', 'the mystery of his will'. He blesses 'him who accomplishes all things according to the counsel of his will'. This is Paul's theme. God has done great things for us, but not simply for our sake.

In saving us, God is working out his own 'plan for the fullness of time', which Paul immediately defines as 'to unite all things in Christ, things in heaven and things on earth' (1:10). In *Colossians* the phrase was, 'to *reconcile* to himself all things...', but here Paul substitutes an illuminating Greek word which means, literally, 'to sum up'. Greek schoolboys doing arithmetic would add *up* a column of figures and place the answer at the *top*; they would 'bring to a head' all the parts of a sum in a unified total. The word was also used in rhetoric for 'summing up', or 'recapitulating', the various points of a speech. Paul means that God's underlying purpose in redeeming men and women is to bring all things again under one uniting head, the headship of Christ, as they had been at the beginning (recall Colossians 1:16–17).

The members of these scattered Asian churches had been a diverse and divisive cross-section of society, Gentiles and Jews, husbands, wives, children, masters, slaves (in *Colossians* he added 'barbarian, Scythian').

Within themselves they had been at odds, followers of 'the spirit at work in the disobedient', 'children of wrath', ignorant, darkened in understanding, callous individualists, each seeking only his own 'desires of body and of mind'.

Among themselves they had been socially divided, 'separated', 'aliens', 'strangers', false, bitter, thieving, slanderous, angry, licentious, covetous, envious of each other.

Beyond themselves they were 'alienated from the life of God', 'without God', 'hostile to God', spiritually insensitive to him ('dead in trespasses and sins'), followers of the 'prince of the power of the air', on the side of the disruptive demonic rulers of this present darkness, 'the spirit-hosts of wickedness in the heavenly places'.

Such is the picture of the world Paul saw as he travelled; over and around it, a fragmented universe. That was God's problem. To reconcile all again under one head, restoring the primeval harmony, was God's ultimate, over-ruling, long-predestined intention.

This breathtaking purpose has moved already towards fulfilment, in the reader's own experience, in their reception of the gospel, their sealing by the Spirit, their faith and love towards the saints. Paul prays they may understand the high aim to which they have been called, and grasp the greatness of that divine power already at work in raising Christ, and in making them 'alive together with Christ', raising them together with Christ, to sit together with Christ in heavenly places above the warring elements. All this has happened, wholly of grace. They are God's workmanship, at one now within themselves, because they are united to Christ, their head.

But more has happened: out of social and spiritual chaos has already arisen a Christian fellowship of these newly-integrated souls, a church. In this church the deepest and most enduring of all the gulfs that separate mankind, that of Jew and Gentile, a gulf at once racial, historical, cultural, religious, and often fanatic, *has already been bridged*. Paul exhausts the language of social division to describe this divine achievement: the separated are brought together, the alienated are reconciled, the strangers are made fellow citizens, those far off are brought near, mere sojourners become full members of God's household, because Christ, who is our peace, has made peace, and preaches peace to the distant and the near.

'The dividing wall of hostility' between Jew and Gentile has been broken down; the law that separated them has been abolished, creating 'a single new humanity' (NEB), neither Jew nor Gentile, but one in Christ. All barriers are down, all feuds ended; those once godless have access by one Spirit unto the Father. Together they are rising as a holy shrine, erected upon the foundation of which Christ is the cornerstone, the whole varied structure firmly bonded together by his Spirit, for a temple, a dwelling-place of God among all men.

This united church, commonwealth, household, temple, is God's second step towards universal reunion. It is fact, not dream — God has done this. The separate churches are agencies of the over-riding purpose, examples of its fulfilment. It is for this magnificent divine aim that Paul is willing to be prisoner 'on behalf of Gentiles' — meaning (apparently) 'to win them' in spite of Jewish opposition. This is the hitherto hidden purpose he wants his readers to grasp clearly — to make the body of Christ universal (3:4–6). This has been God's gracious gift to him, to make men, and even supernatural powers, realize the many-sided wisdom of God. So the Asian Christians are not to lose heart over his present sufferings: it is all utterly worth while.

So Paul prays to the Father, 'from whom his whole family in heaven and on earth derives its name' (NIV), that the one church may be strengthened by the one Spirit, indwelt by the one Christ, rooted in one mutual affection, comprehending together the full dimensions of Christ's surpassing love, and thus being filled with all the fullness of God. To God, whose power can accomplish more than we ever ask or dream, be glory in his church, and in Christ, to all generations. What a prayer!

If all this be true (Paul urges, coming down to earth), our calling in the world is obvious: to maintain, at whatever cost of lowliness, meekness, patience, forbearance, love, the unity of the Spirit in the bond of peace, in this church which is to unify the world. *It is one church*, one body, though varied; imbued with one holy Spirit, with one hope, one Lord, one faith (in contrast with the world's innumerable philosophies), one baptism (Judaism had many washings, the cults many initiations), and one God (against the many gods of separate tribes, groups, trades). Such are the sinews of the church of Christ (compare Colossians 2:19).

Of course, within that unity there are varieties of grace, as Christ gives to each, and varieties of gifts, creating again varieties of ministry. But the ultimate purpose is one, a 'unity of faith and knowledge' that will attain to mature manhood, measured by Christ's own stature. Then we shall no longer be fickle and vulnerable children, prey to deceitful teachers (a side-glance at Colossae?), but growing up into our one head in a united and growing body.

Here Paul turns (as in *Colossians*) to elaborate that elementary convert-training which he could assume would be known even in churches he did not found. In this instance he shows how the pursuit of unity through submission to each other will work out in the different areas of life. In the church, for example, members shall no longer live as once they did, but shall 'put off' the old nature and 'put on' the new. In particular, they are to put away lying, because '*we are members one of another*'; if angry, they are to limit resentment, so giving no opportunity to the devil to divide the fellowship; they are to cease stealing (by living unnecessarily on the church's charity?), working honestly so as to give, instead.

Their conversation is to be pure, helpful, bringing grace to others; and they must do nothing to grieve the holy Spirit dwelling within the fellowship, (by 'lowering the spiritual temperature' as we might say), hindering unity. All antisocial attitudes must be replaced by Christlike ones; all offences against persons (immorality, covetousness) must be avoided. Their lives together should be full of light, wisdom, happy worship. What is forbidden is anything abrasive, divisive; what is commended is outgoing, reconciling. The Christian is to be a *socialized* individual.

So in the Christian home, mutual submission is the rule, as making for peace. Wives take their due place ('obedience' is not in Paul's word); husbands are to love their wives selflessly; their relationship is to be modelled on that of Christ towards his church. Children *are* to be obedient, 'in the Lord', because it is right and brings reward; fathers however are not to provoke children, but teach them the Lord's way. As to daily work, slaves are to serve faithfully, as serving the Lord, and masters to treat their servants in the same way, without threats. Altogether a prescription for a happy and united church, marriage, family and work-relationship, bearing clear testimony to the Christian goal, and God's purpose, of unity under Christ as head.

Paul's final paragraph reads oddly after such exhortations to unity: 'Be armed for conflict!' But Paul was a realist, sharply aware that peace is not gained by talking about peace; that a disruptive spirit was at work in the 'sons of revolt', the demonic powers of division and evil that 'bedevil' the world.

Still using the plural, because Christians fight evil together, Paul recommends the armour of prayer and sound character. The wide leather girdle of the Christian warrior is his integrity, truthfulness through and through. His breastplate, guarding his heart, is devotion to right. His all-important sound shoes (for want of which many a gladiator died), the firm footing of the gospel; his shield against the world's flaming darts of enticement or accusation, is his faith in God. His helmet, guarding his thoughts, is the assured knowledge of ultimate salvation. His only offensive weapon is the sword of the Spirit himself, namely the word of God, which wounds without bitterness and heals as it wounds. (The picture recalls the ancient description of God's own armour — Isaiah 59:16–17.)

So armed, the Christian keeps in touch with his Commander by prayer. To fight and not to pray is to fight alone; but to fight, with God, is to stand firm, and still to be found on the field, steadfast, victorious. Paul asks that such prayer shall always include others who strive likewise for the purpose of God, including himself. After commending Tychicus, he closes with a benediction of peace.

A Manifesto for Our Time

Such is the circular Paul sent around the Asian churches, aware of new fashions of thought and disruptive influences that threatened both the churches and society. We know that he saw the Roman world in danger, as tradition faded, authority was challenged, integrity and trust declined. Yet God had made the world one, and saw that it was good. Sin had destroyed its inner harmony, and God was making it one again, in Christ. Integrated, 'socialized' in themselves, and united in one church across all frontiers, believers must avoid all that frustrates God's purpose. They must be one, remain one, work as one, to realize the world-reconciling aim of God.

Could anything be more apposite, more immediately relevant and uncomfortably practical, than such a call? We grow up into Christ precisely in the measure in which we grow out of self into community, out of isolation into fellowship: so the church becomes firstfruits, model and agency of God's reconciling work.

As Paul makes clear, the variety within the church, both of members and of ministry, is no contradiction of the church's unity, but a contribution to it, catering for all sorts and conditions of Christians. We must not make the richness of Christian tradition and experience an excuse for division. God has set himself the task of reducing all things under one uniting head, namely Christ: and we are his servants.

Suggestions for Group Discussion

1 Let half the group study 1 Corinthians 7 and summarize Paul's view of marriage; let the other half do the same with Ephesians 5:21–33; then compare notes. Which of the two passages is the more relevant to today's situation?

2 *Ephesians* is scripture's greatest argument for church unity across all racial, cultural, and social barriers and amidst all the New Testament churches' diversity. In recent years the emphasis has been upon uniting organizations, ministries, creeds, sacraments, and more recently upon accepting all the differences and fostering fellowship and co-operation. Which does the group think is the right approach to Paul's vision of the church?

3 Ephesians 6:10–18 is the main New Testament justification for our many martial hymns and metaphors. Should we, in these violent days, avoid this language altogether? Are we moderns 'soldiers of Christ' anyway?

CHAPTER 10

Notes to Philippi

Preparatory Reading: Acts 16:11–40, Philippians

Paul had good reason to remember Philippi with pleasure and gratitude. There, after repeated frustration in Asia Minor, his mission had quite suddenly expanded beyond his dreams, with an opening into Macedonia, and so on to the continent of Europe. There a possessed girl-slave had been miraculously set free. There an earthquake had opened the prison, and the jailer's heart.

To crown the brief visit, Paul's first recorded brush against the Roman authorities had ended with the magistrates' public apology, ensuring official protection for the little company of believers Paul was leaving behind, to meet together in the home of hospitable Lydia.

Subsequently, the little congregation at Philippi had sent support 'once and again' to the apostle and his colleagues. There is some reason to believe that Luke was left at Philippi to nourish the work; Paul visited the city at least twice later (2 Corinthians 2:13, Acts 20:6), but further details are lacking.

The church, therefore, had happy memories of Paul, as he had of it. His correspondence with the members is often described as his most calm, affectionate, and full of joy. But this can be overstated. As he writes Philippians 1, Paul is awaiting the verdict upon his life. In chapter 2 he expresses concern over disunity and rivalry among the Philippians, and has to report that Epaphroditus, the church's messenger, has been very ill, 'near to death'. Chapter 3 contains sharp comment on the old Jewish-Gentile controversy, while chapter 4 names certain people whose mutual relationships need help. For all that, notes of peace, gratitude, contentment and joy are struck here and there, and more than once.

It is interesting that Paul's discussion of the Christian reaction to persecution (1:27–30) is offered to a church that had witnessed himself and Silas being whipped and imprisoned. The rivalry of certain women in the church reminds us that the church was founded among a women's prayer group, a woman taking the initiative in inviting the apostles to her home.

The reference to the Christian's 'citizenship' in heaven would be well understood, perhaps ruefully, by Philippians inordinately proud of forming a Roman colony, with Latin street-names, Latin official titles, and a Roman coinage. The readers, and that first visit to them, are evidently present in Paul's mind as he dictates.

Incoherent?

Less welcome, but inescapable in *Philippians* is a certain disjointedness, even incoherence, as though the letter were entirely unplanned. All reads smoothly, and with close adherence to Paul's custom, from 1:1 to 3:1 — Address, Greeting, Thanksgiving, news of his situation, pastoral exhortation and instruction, a notice of future plans, a kindly commendation of their pastor, Epaphroditus, now well enough to return to Philippi, evidently bearing this letter. A 'final' call to rejoice, and we expect the greeting and grace of 4:21–23 to close a brief but heartening letter, very characteristic of Paul.

But that smooth flow is inexplicably interrupted by a sudden and vigorous warning — 'Beware of the dogs, beware of the evil-workers'. And something near self-justification against enemies of the cross of Christ immediately follows. Of these enemies he declares that 'their god is the belly, and they glory in their shame, with minds set on earthly things'.

The whole tone of this outburst contrasts strongly with the tolerant attitude towards rival workers in 1:15–18. Paul reverts to a calmer exhortation that the Philippians 'stand firm', be united, pray, rejoice, and enjoy peace. A 'final' exhortation to think and do as they have been taught ends the brief passage with a simple benediction, 'the God of peace will be with you' (3:2–4:9).

Then comes another new start, and a totally new theme: a very gracious note of thanks for contributions received by the hand of Epaphroditus, closing with a promise of God's reward, a brief doxology, and Amen. After which the greeting and a closing grace (4:21–23) is added somewhat clumsily. This paragraph of grateful acknowledgement could well, of course, belong with 1:1–3:1, if it did not begin so abruptly, and if it did not seem so very much like a late afterthought, when the letter was finally finished, and the memory of Philippi's repeated gifts came inconveniently to mind — just in time!

One might suppose that such an ungracious impression would require rewriting the letter, to say 'Thank you' more promptly. But that would not quite resolve the matter. For Epaphroditus *brought* the gift (4:18), then fell seriously ill; news of this had time to reach Philippi (2:26), but he is now well enough to travel home. Paul really has been slow to express gratitude! Did the church wonder if its pastor had absconded with the gift?

The explanation of this strange patchwork structure of *Philippians* can only be conjectural. 'Constant interruption' is easy to imagine, though Paul could have reread what was written before starting afresh. 'Unexpected news from Philippi' is also conceivable, though Paul does not mention it.

The parallel of '*1 and 2 Corinthians*' makes at least probable the suggestion that more than one letter or note to Philippi has been preserved on the same papyrus, possibly rearranged with minor adjustments of address and greetings, by successive copyists to make a 'tidier' epistle. This may well explain why, in the second century Polycarp speaks of Paul's *letters* to Philippi.

At any rate it would explain the 'delay' in Paul's thanksgiving if, hearing that Paul was in prison and, therefore, in financial need, the Philippian church sent their pastor, with gifts, to cheer up the apostle, and Paul at once sent back his warm thanks, the bearer of that note also reporting the illness of Epaphroditus.

Later, when Epaphroditus recovered, the fuller letter was given him to carry homewards (1:1–3:1 perhaps ending with 4:21–23). There is little in 3:2–4:9 to offer any clue to its date, except that 'forgetting what lies behind and straining forward to what lies ahead I press on . . . Rejoice in the Lord always . . . the Lord is at hand' does not *sound* like a man daily expecting a capital punishment verdict. The sharper tone towards rival preachers, at 3:18–19, suggests some date different from that of 1:15–18, where Paul is tolerant of rivals. On that very slight ground we might tentatively number Paul's notes to Philippi '*1 Philippians*' (4:10–20), '*2 Philippians*' (3:2–4:9), '*3 Philippians*' (1:1–3:1 + ?4:21–23).

Where was Paul?

The greater part of this 'vaguely composite' letter was written from prison while Paul awaited possible death (1:13,17, 20–26, 2:23). The capital charge, and the mention of the Praetorian Guard (1:13, Caesar's household 4:22) were for a long time thought to prove that Paul must have been in Rome. Both arguments are unsound. 2 Corinthians 1:8–10 leaves no doubt that Paul stood in danger of his life, as well as suffering imprisonment, at Ephesus (recall on *Colossians*). And it is now known that the Praetorian Guard were to be found at every provincial Government House, as at Jerusalem (Matthew 27:27). This elite military caste, 'Caesar's Household', was an official 'soldiers' civil service' engaged on the emperor's business in every centre of Roman authority. So powerful was it that, for the safety of the capital, of the total 10,000 no more than 3000 were allowed within its walls at one time (under Augustus). The rest were kept safely scattered, through the empire.

This relieves two real difficulties. If Paul were writing from Rome, at any time after announcing his plans in Romans 15:23–29 (see Acts 19:21, 20:25), then his clear intention to revisit Philippi (Philippians 1:26–27, 2:24) directly contradicts his conviction that his work in the eastern Mediterranean was finished with the carrying of gifts to Jerusalem, and that he should turn westwards to Rome and Spain. Paul could, of course, change his mind; but it would be hard to find a parallel instance of his changing, or abandoning, plans he had 'resolved in the Spirit' (as Luke says). If, however, he is writing *Philippians* during his three years at Ephesus, as he wrote *Colossians, Philemon, Ephesians*, and in the situation he described in 2 Corinthians 1:8–10, then he has not yet made that resolve, and will travel far before he does so.

The other difficulty about a Roman origin of *Philippians* lies in 2:19,23 where Paul hopes to send Timothy to Philippi when the verdict on his own life is known, and to receive news of the church when Timothy returns. From Rome to Philippi and back would take at least two months. Starting after the verdict was announced, Timothy's return must be too late for him to see Paul again. Timothy could reach Philippi from Ephesus and return in a few days.

'1 Philippians'

Paul's 'Thank you' note (4:10–20) reminds us of *Philemon* by the slight humour that playfully borrows from the formal business-receipt of the time (scores have been recovered from the sands of Egypt) the customary Greek phrase for 'paid in full — settled' (4:18), faintly suggesting that the Philippians' gifts were a debt for favours received. But the rest of the note emphasizes that their kind action was an expression of sympathy in trouble, an act of partnership in the gospel, an investment that shall add credit to their account (NIV), a fragrant offering (like incense), an acceptable sacrifice that shall please God.

This useful analysis of Christian generosity is prefaced by remembrance of former kindness ('you had no opportunity' presumably means that Paul could maintain himself until imprisoned); and by a moving Stoic-like affirmation of his inner independence of changing circumstances, enabled by the strength of Christ. A gracious promise that God will repay them whenever they are in need, and a doxology, close the very brief but interesting note.

'2 Philippians'

If 3:2–4:9 really was a second note, its opening lines have obviously been trimmed away. The occasion for it is immediately, not to say passionately, indicated by the reference to 'mutilating the flesh', followed by mention of circumcision. The contemporary letter to Colossae prompts the question whether Paul had just heard Epaphras' report of some who were emphasizing circumcision in his home church, and wishes to equip the Philippians in advance to meet any such danger.

Paul affirms that those who worship in spirit, place all their pride in Christ himself, and put no trust in fleshly grounds of confidence, *are* the true Israel. Paul then recites the fleshly — the human and natural — grounds of confidence he could rightly claim, all of which he had renounced to gain Christ; as he is still willing to renounce everything in order to know Christ, be found in him, and receive the righteousness he bestows, the resurrection he promises. Not that this renunciation gives any ground for pride. Paul insists that he has not yet attained mature completeness. Like an athlete, he strives towards God's prize, and begs that all in training shall strive with him, not yielding any position already attained.

For there are those who are enemies of the cross, headed for destruction, sensual, earthly ('with minds set on earthly things', the other side of the strange teaching in Colossae, see Colossians 3:2–8). The commonwealth of which we are citizens is above, from which we await a Saviour who will change our bodies and subdue all earthly things (a variation on Colossians 3:1–4). Against such trouble-makers and temptations, Paul urges the Philippians to 'stand firm' in the Lord.

Without emphasis, but very directly Paul 'entreats' two Philippian women to find agreement, and asks a 'true yokefellow' to help them do so, for they were fine colleagues, as were Clement, and others whose names God has registered. (The 'yokefellow' would appear to be the leader at Philippi who would receive and read to the assembled members this warning note; the only hints we have would suggest it might be Luke.)

Turning to all the members, Paul urges them to rejoice; to let all men see their evenness of temperament; to remember that 'the Lord is at hand'; and to turn all anxieties into grateful prayers. That will bring peace beyond understanding. They should fill their minds with everything true, pure, lovely, and their lives with the example set before them. That will bring the God of peace ever beside them.

'3 Philippians'

We can be more confident that 1:1–3:1 was a separate and later letter, sent with the recovered Epaphroditus. Paul's opening prayer is full of gratitude for the Philippians' partnership in the gospel (compare 1:5,7,30 and 4:15). His confidence and affection are sure. His prayer is that their enthusiasm will increase in knowledge and discrimination. He then explains his present situation, finding in it a positive advantage in that through his imprisonment his guards have learned the gospel, while fellow Christians have been stirred to greater zeal. Some, it is true, as rivals and partisans, have taken advantage of his absence: but that does not matter if Christ is being proclaimed: he is determined to rejoice.

Paul hopes he will be freed, and not be ashamed even if the outcome of his trial be death. He does not know which to choose, though for him to remain will mean more service for Christ and some advantage for them. So, whatever shall be the end, let the Philippians stand firm in one spirit, one mind, side by side (anticipating the exhortation still to come). And let them not be afraid of their opponents: their fearlessness will be a sign of the persecutors' coming destruction, and of their own salvation. They are partners indeed, in his suffering.

Then comes Paul's main exhortation, presumably evoked by what Epaphroditus has reported. (Have Euodia and Syntyche pursued their rivalry?) Appealing to all the motives of Christian experience (2:1), Paul asks that the Philippians shall 'complete his joy' by being of similar outlook, the same love, of one accord, of united purpose. This will require the exclusion of selfishness, of conceit; the humble acknowledgement that others excel oneself; and a genuine concern for others' interests. Indeed, it requires nothing less than each and all having 'the mind of Christ'.

On the heels of that very practical analysis of the preconditions of Christian unity, and as its chief incentive, comes one of the greatest passages in the Testament. It probably contains lines from an early hymn on the selflessness of Jesus in becoming incarnate, and dying, as the servant of the Lord. Though originally in the 'form' (nature) of God, Jesus, unlike Adam, did not count being 'equal with God' a thing to be grasped after, but 'emptied himself' ('poured out his soul', as Isaiah said the Lord's servant would do), taking the form of a servant (also echoing Isaiah 53).

So Jesus was born in the 'form' (the outward fashion) of men: and even then he humbled himself to be an obedient servant among men, even to the extreme length of dying upon a cross. Therefore, for such selfless obedience, God has made and named him *Lord*, that every knee, in heaven and on earth and in Hades, shall bow before him and acknowledge his right to rule, to the Father's glory. *For that reason*, having that sort of mind within yourselves, learn to get along better together!

Let them, therefore, with like obedience, and as hitherto, diligently work out their salvation-experience to the fulfilment of God's purpose, as God works within them; and do it without raising petty objections or questions, as blameless children of God in an evil generation. So they will offer light and life to all. Thus Paul will be proud of the results of his work; and if his own death completes the sacrifice they are devotedly offering, he will rejoice, as they should too.

Paul mentions his plan to send faithful Timothy with news of the court's verdict, adding a sharp comment on the contrasted selfishness of others. And he highly commends their pastor, speaking of his illness, and the great anxiety it occasioned, his eagerness now to restore him to his people. The exhortation to joy is repeated, with a disclaimer — that to exhort them as he has done before is no trouble to him, and safer for them. It seems probable that the greetings and grace now at 4:21–23 closed this warm-hearted little epistle.

Interest and Value

Each part of this composite epistle has its special significance still. The brief word of thanks has its definition of contentment, and its description of Christian giving. '2 Philippians' is especially memorable for its revelation of Paul's inner attitude to his Jewish inheritance, and his present striving towards the Christian goal. The remarkable tolerance which Paul shows towards his rivals, and the opening of his heart about his present danger, in the first chapter, are self-revelations we would not have missed.

But above all, the prescription for united Christian fellowship at the beginning of chapter 2, leading into that lyrical exposition of the inner meaning of the incarnation and the cross for Jesus, is quite priceless.

The idea of Jesus as the servant of the Lord is to be found often in the New Testament, but nowhere else is it explored so movingly as here — as the all-powerful motive for like selflessness and mutual service in his followers. The passage is worthy to stand beside any in the whole Bible. Here we feel the very pulse of Christianity, the gospel of the self-emptying servant of the Lord who came and suffered for selfish men, and so was made Lord of all. And that passage was miraculously preserved by some zealous scribe, who gathered together the fragments of what Paul had written to Philippi, for the enrichment of the whole church.

Suggestions for Group Discussion

1 As *Thessalonians* helps us in facing another's death, so *Philippians* shows us a great Christian facing his own (most probable) death. Pick out from Philippians 1:19–26, 2:17, (and compare the attitude in 2 Corinthians 1:8–11) the several elements that prepare the Christian to 'make a good death'.

2 We imagine that the first Christians lived in a haze of blessing on the top of spiritual mountains; list in Philippians the references to the unkind rivalry, danger, uncertainty, suffering for Christ's sake, tendency to grumbling, questioning, anxiety, waiting to see God's will, illness, incompleteness of attainment, striving, troubles, unfaithfulness among colleagues, division among friends, hunger, hostile environment, amidst which these first Christians actually lived. When found, set beside these everyday imperfections the recipe for the peace of God, and the presence of the God of peace (4:4–9).

3 4:11–13 (with 1 Corinthians 7:17–24) reminds us that contentment is now the rarest of all the Christian virtues. Let one in the group prepare to speak for eight minutes in praise of contentment, and another for eight minutes criticizing contentment; then let the group decide what it means, and does not mean; what makes for it, and what works against it in our modern life.

CHAPTER 11

A Lengthy Visiting Card

Preparatory Reading: Acts 19:21, Romans 1:8–15, 15:18–29, 5:1–11, ch. 12

Paul had not yet visited Rome, but intended to do so, and writes to say he is coming. The decision was made at Ephesus, that after visiting Jerusalem with the gifts of the churches, he would make for Rome (Acts 19:21, 24:17). This is the plan described in Romans 15:23–29, where we learn that Paul felt he no longer had room for pioneering in the eastern Mediterranean. He intended, therefore, after staying in Rome 'for a little', to pass on to Spain, to resume pioneering in the west.

To ignore the already powerful church in Rome by simply passing beyond them, would be unmannerly and provocative. Beside, Paul hoped 'to be sped on his journey' by the Roman Christians: the phrase means 'to be sent forward with support' (1 Corinthians 16:6, 2 Corinthians 1:16, 3 John 5–8). Paul hoped that the Roman church would supply men, money, prestige, and prayer for his mission to Spain, and writes (between Acts 20:2 and 3?) to prepare the way. The date would be about AD 57. *Romans* seems a very long epistle just to do that, but there were difficulties.

The existence of a very few ancient copies lacking (or confused about) the address 'To all God's beloved in Rome' (1:7,15) shows that the epistle was early counted important enough to adapt as a circular, but there is no reason to doubt that the letter was sent originally to the existing church at Rome. The church had been founded, apparently, by Jews who witnessed events in Judea, possibly at the last Passover of Jesus' ministry, certainly at the following Pentecost. The Jews returned home with their story and so upset the synagogues at Rome that the emperor banished Jews from the city. (Suetonius speaks of 'riots at the instigation of one *Chrestus*' — see Acts 18:2.)

A fourth-century member of the Roman church, Ambrosiaster, says that the church arose among Jews; the Gentiles who joined saw neither miracles nor apostles. A large number of Jews had lived in Rome for nearly a century, and though the church was 'a large body' (Clement), 'an immense multitude' (Tacitus), it is evident that Jews continued to form a large element within it. Several of the subjects of Paul's letter, and his methods of argument, show that Paul was aware of this. At the same time, his emphasis on the gospel preached 'among all nations', and phrases like 'other Gentiles', 'I speak to you Gentiles', show his anxiety to persuade non-Jewish members also.

Suspicions

The difficulties Paul faced in seeking the Roman church's support lay partly in this history. The church owed nothing to Paul: why should they welcome his counsel, or support his schemes, or suppose he could impart anything they lacked? It is significant that having unguardedly suggested that he might, in coming, bestow some spiritual gift to strengthen them, Paul immediately corrects himself with 'that is, that we may be mutually encouraged by each other's faith, both yours and mine'.

Beside, the Roman Christians seem to have felt neglected. If Paul thought and prayed so much about them, why had he not visited them sooner? Was he ashamed to bring his simple gospel to the capital of the empire? The whole of 1:8–17 is defensive: 'Without ceasing I mention you always in my prayers, asking that *somehow, by God's will*, I may *now at last succeed* in coming to you . . . I want you to know that I have often intended to come to you (but thus far have been prevented) . . . I am eager to preach the gospel to you also who are in Rome. For I am not ashamed of the gospel . . .'

There were more serious difficulties, however, than hurt feelings. Continual communication between Rome and Jerusalem by pilgrimage ensured that the Roman church knew of the controversy raised by Paul's offering of salvation to Gentiles by faith in Christ alone. They had the same misgivings as did Christian Jews in Palestine — was not such a message wholly unscriptural, cancelling the divine law? Did it not entirely abolish the age-old prerogative of Israel as the chosen people of God? And was it not morally dangerous to allow loose-living, idolatrous pagans to think they could continue in their sins and yet be saved by faith alone.

And further, everywhere Paul went there was trouble with the Roman authorities; Rome had had enough of that. Paul seemed as anti-Roman as he was anti-Jewish! It was by no means certain, or even probable, that the Roman church would welcome this contentious trouble-maker, or do as he desired.

We know that these difficulties were present to Paul's mind from the space he gives to resolving them. His letter is different in tone from all others except *Ephesians*; he offers no criticism of anything unsatisfactory at Rome, no apostolic commands. Nor is *Romans* a summary of his theology, as is often claimed: the church, the body of Christ, the advent, the Lord's supper, the divinity and pre-existence of Christ, the Christian ministry, God's purpose to reconcile all things, are hardly mentioned in *Romans*, if at all.

Confining himself to Jewish misgivings about himself, Paul writes calmly and at greater length the self-explanation he had written so vehemently and urgently to the Galatians. The same questions demanded the same true answers, though now he has time, reflection, longer experience to help him, and no virulent opponents to contend with.

It is important to define the precise nature of this epistle, since that guides our approach to its message. Essentially, *Romans* was meant to do what the old-fashioned visiting card, or letter of introduction, did — present creden-. tials, announce intended visit and purpose, seek support. In the special circumstances Paul has to be tactful, self-defensive, anticipating objections, and occasionally using the rhetorical method of the 'invisible heckler' to develop his thought without offending his readers. The result is in some ways the most important letter Paul wrote.

A letter so obviously interwoven with Paul's story, so involved with his known attitudes and message, could hardly be other than authentic. No purpose has been alleged for forging such an epistle, no rival claims to authorship are recorded, and citation by Clement of Rome (at the end of the first century) and others during the first quarter of the second century, gave the church good ground for accepting the letter as Paul's.

Modern claims that *Romans* is a totally incoherent muddle put together by different 'editors' are best weighed by careful examination of its closely argued contents. Some uncertainties, dating from ancient times, about the closing passages of the epistle do not affect the general conclusion that the letter is Paul's.

Paul's Case

The slight formality of the opening greeting, and some old phrases (like 'spirit of holiness') suggest Paul is quoting a credal summary of faith, with a familiar strong Jewish flavour that would at once allay any suspicion of his own orthodoxy. Paul passes quickly to a complimentary thanksgiving, with the tactful, defensive statement of his abiding interest in the Roman church and his long-felt intention to visit them (1:1–15).

- *Statement of the Theme* (1:16–17): To the Jew, to be 'in the right with God' was the primary and essential purpose of all religion. Paul defines his gospel as conveying God's power to save all who exercise faith, so revealing the 'righteousness' which God both requires and bestows, 'through faith for faith'. As Habakkuk had foretold, 'the righteous shall live by his *faith*'.
- *The World's Need of Such Righteousness* (1:18–3:20): The Gentiles having inexcusably rejected God, God 'gave them up' to the evils they chose. Judgement is certain, and just, on Jew and Gentile alike; for the Jew, no less than the Gentile, stands condemned as unrighteous, by common repute and by scripture. All are guilty in God's sight.

Paul was not alone in his assessment of Roman society, nor of the poor repute of Jews in some Roman cities. The definition of 'Jew' as one of any race who in heart and spirit keeps the laws of God, is revolutionary, and the heart of Paul's case. The slightly elevated style of this passage may reflect the fact that Paul must often have preached on this subject in the synagogues.

- *God's Provision of Righteousness* (3:21–31): God, however, has not abandoned men entirely, but has intervened to provide a righteousness apart from keeping the law. It is given to faith, and rests upon faith in Christ, alone; it is therefore free, wholly of God's gracious favour. It is based upon the act of God in *setting forth* Christ as an expiation of sin by his blood.

It is probable that Paul has in mind the 'place of expiation', the 'mercy seat' (so the Greek word suggests) standing within the Jewish sanctuary, where 'atoning blood' was sprinkled. In contrast with the hiddenness of that unseen altar, the cross where Jesus died was public, 'set forth' between heaven and earth and among men, for all to see for all time (compare Galatians 3:1). Sin was not condoned, but atoned for by suffering.

So the divine intervention to count men righteous on the ground of faith, where counting them righteous by obedience to the law had failed, was wholly consistent with God's own righteousness — sin is condemned, not excused, though the sinner is 'justified' — a current technical term for counting men righteous.

God in his forbearance had 'passed over' former sins; now by setting forth Christ he proves that he himself is righteous, while counting righteous the sinful who believe in Jesus. This method of salvation totally excludes boasting, *self*-righteousness, because faith and not works is its principle. And it is universal: God deals with Jews and Gentiles on the one basis — faith in Christ. 'Does all this overthrow the law? We shall show that it upholds the law!'

This is a crucial passage for understanding Paul's gospel. Its meaning depends very much upon what is implied by 'faith in Christ', which Paul will explain later. (See also Chapter 13: Paul's Christianity.) Meanwhile, Paul deals with the Roman church's misgivings.

- *The Faith Method of Attaining Righteousness Defended* (4–8:4):
  - *(i) As Fitting God's Known Ways* (4): Salvation by faith is fully in accord with the experience of Abraham (who was counted righteous on account of his faith, long before either circumcision or the law was given), and of David, whose sins were not accounted to him — the equivalent of being counted righteous. Salvation by faith is, therefore, guaranteed to all who share Abraham's faith, whether Jews or Gentiles. What was that faith, but a wholehearted belief that God could give life

to the dead (in the birth of Isaac), and create things that did not then exist (like the new Israelite nation)? But that is precisely the content of *Christian* faith in Christ's resurrection and the emergence of the new Israel, the church. Such has been God's way from the beginning!

- (*ii*) *As Actually Conveying Salvation* (5:1–11): Being counted righteous on the ground of faith, we do in practice have peace with God, access to God's presence and favour (denied to Jews by the curtain in the shrine), and the hope of regaining that reflected glory of God which Adam lost.

We have, also, joy in suffering, as producing endurance, character, and hope — hope already doubly guaranteed to us by the inpouring of divine love and the gift of God's Spirit.

We have, further, assurance of salvation from the final wrath. All is given to the ungodly, to enemies, for it was while we were such that God loved, Christ died, and rose to save us by his life.

To crown all, we have joy in God himself, being now at one with him. The faith method of attaining righteousness does work, as every Christian testifies.

- (*iii*) *As Eminently Reasonable* (5:12–21): Christ forms 'a sort of parallel' with Adam, and Christian salvation obtained through Christ's obedience forms 'a sort of parallel' with the sin and death that entered the world through Adam's disobedience. Paul greatly complicates his illustration by at the same time drawing out six similarities and six differences between what happened through Adam and what happens through Christ; and by leaving one sentence unfinished.

Paul is not arguing against man's need of salvation, but offering another example of the timeless consequences of one man's act, to show that Jewish theology itself accepted the principle of 'one for all'. If rabbis argued that ruin came through one man, why should not salvation come through one, also? Jewish minds would feel the weight of a biblical parallel, or 'type'.

- (*iv*) *As Ethically Sound, Safe, and Effective* (6): Righteousness by faith in Christ, alone, did not leave Gentiles or Jews to 'continue in sin', because faith in Christ's dying and rising for us includes a union with Christ so close that as Christ died to sin so the Christian, *by accepting what Christ did for him*, dies with Christ, to sin and all evil.

The Christian cannot claim that Christ died for his sins without taking his own place with Christ upon the cross ('together-crucified with him' is Paul's phrase); and as Christ rose from the dead to new life, so the Christian, by accepting Christ, rises to new life with him. The man of faith *cannot* continue in sin; his faith-union with Christ precludes it.

This ethical death-resurrection involved in faith in the dying-rising

Lord is dramatically expressed in baptism, and must be constantly re-affirmed thereafter. Its consequences are freedom from the 'reign' and tyranny of sin (recall 5:6, 14, 17, 21), life henceforth in the bond-service of righteousness, and immortality.

- (v) *As Succeeding Where Law Failed* (7:1–8:4): The other Jewish objection, that righteousness attained by faith in Christ, alone, annuls the sacred law, Paul answers with personal testimony. Death with Christ sets the man of faith free from law, as well as from sin (Paul's illustration of the widow just misses his point!).

Though a Pharisee devoted to the law, Paul has to confess law failed to save him. The law was 'good' in exposing sin within; Paul recalls his passage from childhood innocence to sinful desire, resulting in the adult's bitterly divided self, in terms of the Adam story (9–11), and insists that the law itself was holy (7:7, 10,12–14, 22, 8:3).

The failure is the fault of sin dwelling in his own carnal nature. What the law forbade, sin craved; so under the law he was left wretched and helpless. But in Christ the old carnal nature dies, condemnation is removed, and a new 'law' or rule, that of 'the Spirit of life in Christ Jesus' replaces that of sin and death — an invasive moral dynamic that transforms the divided self.

Thus what the law failed to do, God does, first by condemning sin in Christ's death, and then by substituting the rule of the Spirit working powerfully from within, for the rule of laws imposed from without. The moral requirements of divine law have still to be fulfilled, but 'by inspiration, not regulation'.

- *The Faith Method of Attaining Righteousness Defended Positively* (8:5–39): Leaving the defensive stance, Paul asserts the spiritual results of being accounted righteous by faith in a full description of life under the rule of the Spirit. The carnal mind is replaced by a spiritual mind, directed to spiritual ideals. Assurance of sonship replaces that of slavery, and with sonship, the hope of further inheritance. This hope includes universal regeneration, Nature herself being delivered from futility.

Life under the Spirit ensures also effectual praying, as the intercession of the Spirit aids our own; while the Spirit makes all experience work towards the supreme goal of making those who co-operate with God Christlike, so recapturing the lost glory. Life under the Spirit, having God 'with us', means unassailable security, against all accusation (since it is God who acquits us), and against all adversity, since no experience, or enmity, can separate us from the love of God in Christ.

- *The Faith Method of Attaining Righteousness and Jewish Privilege* (9–11): In reply to the further Jewish objection, that Paul's universal gospel denies the unique Jewish prerogative of divine election and destiny, Paul affirms his intense patriotism (echoing Moses, Exodus 32:32), and names nine 'advantages' of being a Jew. God has not broken his word to Israel (in saving Gentiles): it is for God to decide who are 'Israel', as he did in choosing Isaac and not Ishmael, Jacob and not Esau, though all four were 'children of Abraham'. Selection, not automatic inheritance, is the principle of 'election'.

God is sovereign and free; man has no right to question him. If God chooses Gentiles also (as Hosea foresaw), or even rejects some of Israel (as Isaiah foresaw), that is his right. Thus believing Gentiles have attained the righteousness which unbelieving Israelites missed.

Paul deeply desires Israel's salvation; they have great zeal for God, but it is unenlightened — seeking righteousness by law-keeping. Christ ended that way. Thus Israel's rejection is her own fault. By a running commentary on familiar Old Testament phrases, Paul argues that Israel had ample opportunity to receive the simple gospel available to Jew and Gentile alike. Hence the need to preach it, giving opportunity to all, although scripture foresaw both Israel's unresponsiveness and Gentile faith.

Yet Israel's rejection is only partial and temporary; a remnant is to be saved. And one good result of Israel's unbelief has been Gentile opportunity — how much greater the blessing when Israel is saved. Let not Christian Gentiles, therefore, boast over the Jews; Gentiles have been grafted into God's tree in place of Israel's withered branches, and can be pruned out again; so let them show no arrogance. All Israel will be saved; God can make disobedience the occasion for mercy, for Gentiles now, for Israel in the end. Such a vision, based on God's original promise to the patriarchs, moves Paul to a doxology.

The abrupt beginning and self-contained argument of 9–11, and the fact that it can be read without the preceding and following chapters, while chapter 8 reads smoothly on to 12, all suggest that Paul has pulled from his pocket a much-used synagogue sermon, to answer an objection he has met so often before. Paul makes the best of an embarrassing problem: God's promise to Israel must stand, yet Israel crucified the Messiah. Only God decides who *are* Israel, and in mercy has included all sharing Abraham's faith. Let not Gentiles presume on that mercy. Israel's rejection is partial, temporary, and her own fault, but in the end Israel will return to faith. And all is according to scripture.

- *Exhortation to Life Expressing this New Righteousness* (12:1–15:13): By continually re-affirming their death to sin and surrender to the Spirit, men of faith must prove the faith-way of righteousness by *being* righteous:
  - (*i*) *In the church*, at intelligent sacrificial worship, that involving body,

106

mind and will; in mutual and willing service, exercising God's gifts; in true fellowship, selfless, supportive, prayerful, hospitable; and before outsiders, not vengeful but sympathetic, humble, peaceable, overcoming all evil with good.

- (*ii*) *In the State,* Paul applies to Rome the ancient Judaist concept of the theocratic State, where all authority is God's, merely delegated to officials to keep order. Christians, as good citizens, have nothing to fear; they should actively support the civil authority with taxes, dues, respect, and honour. This counsel closely resembles that given to Jews living in pagan cities, and recalls Jesus's words about rendering to Caesar what is Caesar's. The paragraph had special importance to those living under Caesar's shadow in Rome, and also as meeting any suspicion that he himself was subversive. So far Paul has benefited from Rome's civil order; when Rome persecuted, Paul would resist to death.

- (*iii*) *In Society,* Paul urges, remember the command to love, live in full daylight with nothing to hide, and be ready for conflict. Rome offered temptations to compromise with a cultured society (contrast Corinth). 'Pay them all their dues' applies to neighbours as well as officials; the greatest debt is to love, which fulfils all social requirements (again echoing Jesus), Christ's Day is approaching — be always ready.

- (*iv*) *Among Christian Brethren:* To assert freedom from law is to open the way for endless variations in behaviour on the less fundamental moral questions, such as vegetarianism, sabbatarianism, teetotalism; and so to foster disunity. 'Weak' (tender-minded) Christians have doubts, scruples, fears, and to them what they think is wrong *is* wrong, and spiritually harmful. 'Strong' (tough-minded) Christians have few scruples, assert their freedom in Christ, and feel contempt for the weak. The weak watch the strong, criticize them, sometimes imitate, to their own wounding of conscience. Paul indicates five principles of Christian freedom: avoid disputes; support the brother who differs from you, allowing his freedom; let each answer to Christ, only; the individual conscience and conviction must be held sacred; acknowledge equal sincerity in all.

But Paul adds five principles by which love tempers freedom:

Love feels responsibility for all for whom Christ died

Love admits that what a brother thinks will harm him is what matters — not what it thinks (his conscience limits your actions)

Love keeps a sense of proportion as to what is vital, what trivial

Love accepts varying standards, insights, robustness or tenderness of faith within one fellowship

Love realizes that the two types are not equally placed. The weak think the strong are sinning, the strong think the weak are merely silly: but the weak are the more vulnerable, so the strong must carry the weak (by forbearance, self-discipline, some surrender of freedom), not the weak carry the strong. If that seems to ask too much, remember Christ pleased not himself.

Paul speaks of himself as among the strong, and his discussion obviously aims at helping the weak to become strong, while protecting them meanwhile. It seems probable that Paul had experienced this kind of disunity, especially between Jews and Gentiles, in other churches, and expects it to arise also at Rome. But similar differences could arise between strict and careless Jews, between cultured and uncultured Gentiles; so in *Romans* the discussion is conducted in general terms, although in 15:7–13 the Jewish-Gentile basis of the difficulty comes to the surface.

• *Paul's Plans, Greetings, Warnings and Doxology:* A tactful tribute, an explanation of his writing to them, and a reiteration of his plans, reveal some trepidation about his personal safety in Judea, asking for prayers. Paul closes with a brief benediction (15:33). Paul's fears were amply justified; he came at last to Rome aged by long imprisonment, in chains, his active career at an end.

A doxology, 'Now to him who is able to strengthen you... to the only wise God be glory for evermore through Jesus Christ! Amen.' occurs in ancient manuscripts of *Romans* in three different places, or not at all (16:25–27, 14:23; both places; 15:33). Another brief benediction occurs after 16:20 or 16:23 or both.

A few copies of *Romans* end at chapter 14, with or without the doxology. No convincing explanation has been found, but with the absence of the address at 1:7,15, it seems probable that at some time copies were adapted as circulars for other churches, though why the break should occur at 14, or the doxology and benediction vary in position, remains unexplained.

Appended to chapters 1–15 is a recommendation of Phoebe, a deaconess of the church at Cenchreae near Corinth, with a request that she be helped in every way. This is followed by very warm greetings and reminiscences addressed to more than 28 of Paul's friends — an illuminating list. A serious warning follows, against those who oppose the doctrine which the readers have been taught, with a condemnation of their motives and flattery. Timothy and six others, with Tertius the secretary, add their greetings, and the variably-placed doxology closes the chapter in most copies.

Several questions arise. How could Paul recommend Phoebe to Rome while he himself remained in need of introduction? How could Paul know so many people in Rome, their relationships, histories, and house-groups

— 'Had Paul's friends migrated in a body to the capital?' And if so, was *Romans* really necessary, with so many able to speak for him? The warning (17–20) seems to come very late in the epistle, and is quite unrelated to its great arguments.

Some find the doxology very unlike Paul, and think it *could* have been 'a dozen golden Pauline phrases' gathered from his correspondence to compose a suitable ending to the whole collection of Paul's letters, when *Romans* came last in the arrangement.

The frequent communication between Corinth and Ephesus, via Phoebe's Cenchreae, the three years Paul spent in Ephesus, the special reference to his first convert in Asia (5), and the mention of Prisca, Aquila, Timothy, well known at Ephesus, all suggest that chapter 16 was sent to a church where Paul's recommendation would be weighty, his friends numerous — namely Ephesus.

The warning, too, recalls Paul's final words to the Ephesian elders (Acts 20:29). Did Paul send a copy of *Romans*, without the localized details, to the church at Ephesus, accompanied by this recommendation and greetings to friends *there*? Though the ancient copies of *Romans* offer no manuscript support, the suggestion is persuasive, but not proved.

Permanent Value

It seems superfluous to ask the permanent value of a letter like *Romans*, one of the foundation title-deeds of original Christianity. It has been contended that this epistle inspired and guided through Augustine the transition from the Roman Empire to later Europe; through Luther, created the Protestant Reformation; through John Wesley, stirred the British Evangelical Awakening; and through Karl Barth brought the Biblical renaissance to sceptical Europe in the twentieth century.

At least parts of chapters 3, 5, 6, 7, 8, 12, 13 and 14 may fairly be said to have been the illumination and nourishment of thousands of Christian lives, ever since they were written. Not even the somewhat stiff and opaque translation of the 'Authorised/King James Version' has been able to quench its kindling thought and infectious faith.

This is not to deny that the letter has left some intractable problems for the later church. We wish that Paul had dwelt as long upon explaining God's 'putting forth Christ as expiation' as he did on the place of the Jew in the divine purposes. Even in that three-chapter examination, he has hardly spoken the final word!

Paul's doctrine of civil obedience to established authority is not the New Testament's definitive position, nor Paul's own when the State turned persecutor and Satanic (as John the Seer saw it). And what is the Christian to do when rebellion seems a social duty?

Much in his paragraphs on faith, the relation of faith and baptism, the experience of the Spirit, the regeneration of Nature, fine as they are, leave us asking for more. But this merely means we wish he had written a book, not simply a request for help in evangelizing Spain.

Yet *Romans* is invaluable. Autobiographically it is a treasure-house. It reveals more of Paul's inmost attitudes, of the psychological background of his conversion, his frustrated hopes and plans, his intense patriotism, both as Jew and as Roman freeman, his rationale of salvation, and (whether chapter 16 is part of *Romans* or an accompanying note) of his warm friendships, than any other letter, or all the rest together.

As a commentary upon *Galatians*, this epistle is illuminating; while its vision of God's *ongoing* judgement in history, its sense of the power of evil, and of the Spirit who delivers from it, its outline of a philosophy of history in 9–11, and the discussion of Christian freedom tempered by love, are all important contributions to Christian thought. We could hardly expect more of a visiting card.

Suggestions for Group Discussion

(*Romans* itself starts a dozen questions: the following suggestions are hardly necessary.)

1 Romans 14:1–15:6 shows the pastor Paul at his best, handling disagreements between tough-minded and tender-minded Christians over 'opinions' about drink, meat, how to use Sunday, etc. Let a member of the group read out 14:10, another 14:14, another 14:15, another 15:1 — and let discussion proceed. But did Paul really solve the problem of contentious Christians? Is there a better way?

2 Romans 13:1–7 rests upon Old Testament ideas of theocracy, though here applied to the Roman authorities. Is the passage relevant to democracy, where the basis of authority is the will of the majority, not the will of God? Does verse 2 apply under all political regimes?

3 Why was 15:28,29 (so definitely expressed) never fulfilled (so far as history knows)? What does that teach us about our own plans for Christ's work, or for our own?

CHAPTER 12

Pauline Afterthoughts?

Preparatory Reading: Acts 16:1–3, Philippians 3:19–24, 1 Timothy 1–3, 2 Timothy 1:3–7, 2:1–8, Titus 2

The three personal letters which in our New Testament complete Paul's writings are probably among the least read parts of the Testament (along with *2 and 3 John, Jude, 2 Peter*). Yet they contain a number of interesting passages — Paul's 'last words', apparently, in readiness for death; a glimpse into Timothy's home background; a fine definition of the essence of the gospel (Titus 3:4–7); a memorable lesson on Christian discipline (2 Timothy 2:1–7), and a number of 'faithful sayings' which encapsulate basic Christian principles.

More important, these three 'pastoral epistles', as they have long been called because of their contents, bring the New Testament closer to the church we know today than does any other part. The atmosphere of these letters, the church organization, the longer perspective, even the temptations faced, are such as we can identify with. In spite of this, 'the pastorals' are not very familiar to many people, and it will be useful to summarize their contents, and recall the men to whom they are addressed, before asking further questions about their purpose.

Timothy was of Lystra, the son of a Greek father and a Jewish mother; *2 Timothy* records the sincere faith of his grandmother Lois and his mother Eunice, and his early training in the Jewish scriptures. Nevertheless, in view of his Gentile father, it was advisable that Timothy be circumcised when he joined Paul's party, to forestall Jewish antagonism.

Converted by Paul, Timothy was a little later 'well reported of' by the elders of the church at Lystra and took the place of John Mark as a personal attendant to the missionary party through Asia, Troas, and Macedonia.

Left behind at Beroea Timothy rejoined Paul at Athens, was sent back to Thessalonica, and rejoined Paul again at Corinth. He is next mentioned at Ephesus with Paul, where he was sent into Macedonia. Later still he is with Paul again in Macedonia and travels to Corinth. He is with Paul at Troas on the last fateful journey to Jerusalem. Timothy is named with Paul in sending, or in adding his greetings to, five or six epistles, and apparently delivered

1 Corinthians. Paul requires that there he shall be put at ease, and not despised (1 Corinthians 16:10–11).

In the pastoral letters Timothy is at some time left at Ephesus, at another called to rejoin Paul 'soon'. We learn, too, of his need of wine for some stomach ailment, and of his frequent ill health. From the tone of the letters addressed to him, as well as that warning to Corinth, we infer that Timothy needed encouragement and stiffening of resolve from time to time, and further advice to let *no one* despise his youth (1 Timothy 4:12). Yet Paul was greatly attached to his 'son in the Lord', who served him 'as a son with a father'. Paul says to the Philippians 'I have no one like him... genuinely anxious for your welfare... Timothy's worth you know'; and writing to Corinth Paul calls him 'my beloved and faithful child in the Lord'. At some time unknown, Timothy suffered imprisonment (Hebrews 13:23).

Titus also was a convert of Paul's, from Greek (or possibly mixed) parentage (Galatians 2:3). He accompanied Paul from Syrian Antioch to Jerusalem, and was sent to Corinth three times, to organize the collection of gifts for Judea, to deal with disorders there, and to convey Paul's 'reconciling letter' when the trouble was over.

The letter addressed to Titus speaks of his being left at Crete, and being called to Nicopolis; *2 Timothy* tells of his going to Dalmatia. From *2 Corinthians* we gather that he was tactful, prudent, firm, and devoted, just the man for a difficult task at Corinth or Crete. It is very strange that so fine and so busy a man is never mentioned in *Acts*. A brilliant speculation — it is no more — would make the unknown 'brother famous among all the churches in the gospel' (so Greek of 2 Corinthians 8:18) none other than Luke, and the reference to *the gospel* conceivably to an early version of Luke's gospel; if all that were true, then 'the brother' means 'brother of Titus' — and Titus' absence from *Acts* is explained!

Pastoral Instructions

In *1 Timothy*, after a somewhat unusual address and greeting, Paul urges Timothy to remain at Ephesus to oppose false teaching involving myths and genealogies, threatening to displace 'the divine training that is in faith', namely 'love issuing from a pure heart, a good conscience, and sincere faith'. For certain ignorant persons, desiring to be teachers of the law, have initiated vain discussion. The law is good *for the lawless*, according to the gospel with which Paul was entrusted, being counted faithful although formerly a persecutor and foremost of sinners — a clear example of the patience of Christ. Timothy is again charged, with a reminder of the inspired call that came to him, to keep a good conscience; some have not done so, and have come to shipwreck, being delivered to Satan.

'First of all' Paul urges that prayers be made for all in authority, that Christians may live peaceable lives, since God wishes all to be saved. So Christ gave himself a ransom for all, as Paul was appointed to testify, and to teach to Gentiles. Paul urges, too, that women be modest in dress, adorned with good deeds, learning submissively, never teaching men, because Eve was deceived and transgressed; but women will be saved through childbearing if they behave well.

Paul next lists the qualifications required in 'bishops' (Greek 'overseers') and in deacons, temptations arising from their work being clearly in mind. These instructions are given lest Paul be delayed, that Timothy may know how to proceed in the church. The rise of false teaching about marriage and diet was clearly foretold; Timothy must instruct well, avoiding myths, exercising himself in godliness, and setting an example in behaviour, worship, and teaching. Advice follows on how to treat older and younger people, and how to provide wisely for widows, 'enrolling' only the older, encouraging the younger to remarry.

Faithful elders should be provided for, and no accusations against them lightly received, but those who sin publicly must be rebuked. These 'rules' must be kept; Timothy must deal wisely with people, and sensibly with his own ailments. Slaves must learn to work conscientiously, even for indulgent Christian masters. Those who deny such duties are conceited, ignorant, contentious, depraved, avaricious to the point of spiritual peril. Timothy must shun such attitudes, laying hold of eternal life. The rich are to be warned. Timothy is to avoid godless talk and false knowledge. 'Grace be with you' is a very abrupt ending to a mixed, and largely incoherent, epistle.

2 *Timothy* is scarcely more connected, and suggests a young pastor under some pressure. It begins with warm thanksgiving for Timothy and remembrance of his family, with a call to rekindle the gift of God, and not to be timid or ashamed, but willing to suffer for the gospel, for which Paul was appointed a preacher, and is suffering unashamed. Timothy is to follow the pattern of truth already learned. All in Asia deserted Paul, except hospitable Onesiphorus, who has served him in Rome and in Ephesus.

Timothy, then, is to be strong, and teach, accepting suffering, patiently awaiting results. 'Christ is risen: I am fettered, but God's word is not!' The promise of God is sure. So charge men to avoid disputes. Timothy is to be a good workman with the truth, avoiding godless chatter which ruins people, like Hymenaeus (again) and Philetus. The superscription on God's seal is trustworthy: 'The Lord knows his own', and 'Let his own depart from iniquity'. Be a noble vessel in God's house; shun passion, aim at faith, love, peace; avoid controversy, be gentle in teaching, to win again the erring.

In the last days all kinds of hypocrisy will arise, and plausible religious rogues, but Timothy has watched Paul's example, and has learned the scriptures from childhood: let him adhere to what he knows. Paul charges Timothy again to preach truth, patiently, in days when people do not want it. For Paul is ready for death and for his reward. Timothy should come to him soon: others have deserted, or have gone on other tasks. Alexander did harm — God will repay him. None stood with Paul at his first answer, but God delivered him, and will do so. Greetings for others, and from some friends, with a brief grace, conclude another very disjointed letter.

Paul's letter to Titus begins with a very elaborate introduction of himself, asserting his commission as a preacher. Titus is reminded that he was left at Crete to put things in order and appoint elders in every town, men blameless, monogamous, with good children. For the overseer must pass various tests of faith and character. Empty talkers abound, especially Jews, and the Cretans are a bad lot. Titus must be firm; corrupt professors of religion are detestable.

Titus is to handle wisely older and younger Christians, himself a model of Christian character and teaching, to avoid outsiders' criticism. Slaves are to be submissive and honest. For God's grace appeared in order to train us in godliness, and to await the coming of Christ. Titus should remind his people to submit to the authorities, to work honestly, to avoid quarrelling, and to be courteous, remembering what we all were until the goodness of God saved us.

Let Titus insist on such duties, so that believers may apply themselves to good deeds. He should avoid controversies, genealogies, quarrels about the law, and shun the persistently factious, self-condemned, and perverted. Titus is to come to Nicopolis, where Paul will winter. He is to help forward Zenas and Apollos. 'Let our people learn to apply themselves to good deeds' and to help cases of urgent need. Greetings, and a grace, end a pedestrian letter, full of demands rather than encouragement.

Disturbing Impressions

Seeking clues to the background of these letters (as always, the only sure guide to their meaning), we cannot avoid a number of troublesome impressions:

- (i) *A marked change in atmosphere* distinguishes the pastorals from Paul's earlier letters and from Luke's picture of the church in *Acts*. The earlier exuberance, overflowing zeal, freedom of initiative, variety of expression, and immediate sense of divine guidance, are nowhere in the pastoral letters. Instead we meet repeated exhortations of a challenging, driving nature — commands, instructions to behave well, lists of virtues to strive after, 27 times; 'a good conscience' six times; 'warfare' three times; 'rules, duties, be strong, suffer', nine times. Added to these are 13 prohibitions, attitudes and ideas to be strictly avoided.

Fifty-eight such moral jolts and reprimands in 242 verses could not but lend a hectoring tone to these letters. Even more significantly, Paul's frequent words for 'joy', 'rejoice' (51 times elsewhere), and inner 'peace' (34 times elsewhere) are in the pastorals reduced to once, and four times (three times in formal greetings) respectively. While the holy Spirit, never far from Paul's mind in other letters, is mentioned in relation to the inner experience of the Christian only in Titus 3:5, and possibly at 2 Timothy 1:7. This is all a far distance from Romans 8, Galatians 5, Acts 2–4: but how far, in time?

- (*ii*) *A marked change in appointment to service* is equally clear. In *Acts* and 1 Corinthians 12–14, ordinary believers are divinely endowed with various 'gifts' of speech, prophecy, healing, government, teaching, ecstatic speech, equipping them *as the Spirit wills* for positions in the church.

In the pastorals, all emphasis falls upon tests to be applied, qualifications to be required, of aspirants to office, 15 for bishops, 12 for deacons, eight for 'enrolled widows' (apparently dedicated to welfare work), in *1 Timothy*; three for elders and 13 for bishops (if they are other than elders) in *Titus*; *and not a single mention of the holy Spirit in the whole process of selection.*

The number of church officers has grown; the authority of the apostolic delegates (Timothy and Titus) to appoint elders (in place of the earlier election by fellow-members, Acts 16:2, 1 Timothy 4:14, Acts 13:1–3) is emphasized; a superior, presiding bishop may be indicated by the Greek expression 'the bishop' in 1 Timothy 3:2, Titus 1:7, contrast Philippians 1:1; charismatic prophets have disappeared, but are remembered (1 Timothy 4:14); the right ordering of the ministry is for the first time given prior attention. A duly selected and disciplined hierarchy, maintained by the members, has replaced the charismatic ministry of the early years. Institution has replaced inspiration as the controlling ethos of the church — in barely 10 years?

- (*iii*) *The central Christian experience has changed, too.* The pastoral epistles know nothing of faith as so uniting the Christian to Christ that he dies and rises with him, a transformed servant of righteousness, freed from the power of sin and brought under the rule of the Spirit, who produces in him the graces of Christian character and the likeness of Christ. (Not all was accomplished at once, even in Paul's earlier representation; striving towards the goal was still necessary, but the crucial work was done, and salvation had only to be 'worked out'.)

In the pastoral letters all is different. Faith is essentially sound doctrine, 'the divine training that is faith', as opposed to 'speculations' (1 Timothy

1:4), a 'mystery' that deacons must 'hold' with a clear conscience, as Paul had 'kept the faith'. Timothy must 'fight the good fight of faith', and not 'miss the mark as regards the faith'. Even the fine statement of Titus 3:4–7 reads like the recital of a creed rather than the memory of an experience.

Other uses of the word can be found in the epistles, but this is the predominant one: faith as 'sound' or 'healthy' doctrine (someone finds 51 references to that idea!), *to which must be added* sound character, by conscientious effort, diligent self-discipline, 'exercise in godliness', cultivation of virtues, right attitudes, a 'godly and respectable manner of life'; by toiling and striving, taking heed, aiming high, guarding what is entrusted, and doing our best. It is not a direct contradiction of Paul's earlier exuberant, joyful, overflowing love for Christ, but it is very different. The passionate apostle has become carefully orthodox, a sober churchman (or worse still, a mere lecturer on religion) instead of an inspired and inspiring evangelist. In a few short years?

- (*iv*) *The lowered spiritual temperature* is revealed in other ways, too. Ministers might now be drunkards, and lovers of money, teaching for base gain; congregations with itching ears choose the preachers they prefer; some try to make their godliness pay dividends; others leave poor relations to the care of the church's common purse.

The urgency of the advent hope, which made Paul advise that it was better not to marry as 'the appointed time was very short', has now faded somewhat, though the hope of his appearing is still cherished. Younger widows now should marry and bear children, and the advice has a ring of sorry experience about it (1 Timothy 5:11–15). And Timothy should teach what he has learned from Paul to faithful men who shall be able to teach others, making a teaching chain of four generations. So has the perspective lengthened, the excitement that disturbed the Thessalonians subsided, and the warning to be ready at all times as 'children of the Day' lost its gravity.

Other time-notes in the pastorals might illuminate this change, if only they were clearer. We read of 'later times', 'last days' as though they had arrived, or were imminent. By 2 Timothy 1:17 Paul can speak of being in Rome (which could mean any time after Acts 28:14). But this would be *at least* 12 years (some would say 17) since Paul first engaged Timothy. That makes 'Let no one despise your youth... shun youthful passions' read strangely. Was Timothy still a young man in these 'later times'?

- (*v*) *The teaching opposed seems to be later rather than earlier,* since it appears concerned with fringe questions rather than central issues. The Judaist basis of the 'different doctrine' is evident in references to the law, with its endless moral dilemmas, to circumcision, to 'godless and silly Jewish myths' (? Haggadoth, fables, instructive legends read at devotional gatherings, preserved in the Talmud), to 'endless genealogies'. (Philo calls the period from the creation to the giving of the law 'the Genealogies', and the 200 BC *Book of Jubilees* reveals the fanciful 'spiritual' use sometimes made of them.)

'Human commandments' probably refers to 'the tradition of the elders' about trivialities of behaviour. Certain untrained 'teachers of the law', not really understanding what the law is for, appear to be taking advantage of the freer Christian worship (compared with the synagogue, where they could not take part) to air 'speculative' and 'godless chatter' about words. They are empty talkers, insubordinate, delighting to start 'stupid, senseless controversies'. They do not appear to be imposing circumcision, or legalism, only debating their significance. They also mislead weak, persuadable women, unable to learn the truth.

Whether more than this uneducated fringe of Judaism infiltrating the church is implied, it is hard to decide. Gnostic influence has been detected in the prohibition of marriage, and of some foods, in deceitful speech and 'doctrines of demons', in professing to know God while denying him in deeds, in contradictions falsely called knowledge, and the 'morbid craving for controversy'. But some, if not all of these features might be found in Judaist sects (the Essenes, for example), and there is no reference in the pastorals to serious gnostic heresy concerning the person of Christ (unless 1 Timothy 2:5 is a distant allusion); nor is there serious theological counter-argument, but rather ridicule and contempt, dismissing the teaching as 'old wives' tales' and empty chatter.

The consequence of this teaching is not heresy but unprofitable controversy, and there is hope that with *gentle* teaching the offenders may come to know the truth. Timothy must hold to the truth long known, and treasure the scriptures. There is no help here to date the pastorals, except a general impression of lateness.

- (*vi*) *And is there not change here in the apostle himself?* Unfortunately, the attentive and candid reader of the pastorals is gradually made aware that the character of the apostle no longer exhibits the gentle patience of that long discussion over the weak and the strong (in *Romans*), or the tolerance of rivals in *Philippians*. Now we read 'If anyone does not agree ... he is puffed up with conceit, he knows nothing ... As for a man who is factious, have nothing to do with him ... empty talkers and deceivers must be *silenced* ... Their very minds and consciences are corrupted ... they are detestable ... unfit for any good deed ... pretentious and conscienceless liars ... perverted, sinful, and self-condemned ... fools!'

Though Paul tells Timothy to be kindly to everyone, forbearing ... correcting opponents with gentleness, he himself here offers no instruction to the opponents, no persuasion, but only condemnation descending towards abuse.

Similarly, the self-depreciation of 'Not I but grace... Not I but Christ... I am a fool in glorying...' has given place to 'Christ judged me faithful by appointing me to his service... You have observed my teaching, conduct, aim in life, faith, patience, love, steadfastness, persecutions... sufferings, endurance... I have fought the good fight... for me the crown'.

Curiously, Paul reminds Timothy, of all people, *three times*, that he had been appointed by God a preacher, apostle, teacher. The repeated complaints, 'Demas has deserted *me*... All deserted *me*... (May it not be charged against them!)... Alexander the coppersmith did *me* great harm... All in Asia turned away from *me*...' do not sound at all like the earlier Paul, concerned only for the cause; while the naming of Hymenaeus and Alexander ('whom *I* have delivered to Satan'), Phygelus and Hermogenes, Hymenaeus (again) and Philetus, so personalizing the opposition, is not at all the way he dealt with the incestuous man at Corinth ('*you* are to deliver to Satan').

The 'excuse' offered for his former persecuting, 'I had acted ignorantly in unbelief... I received mercy for this reason, that in me, as the foremost, Jesus Christ might display his perfect patience...' is of course correct as to fact, but somehow out of harmony in feeling compared with the penitent prayer long afterwards in Acts 22:19, and the devoted 'He loved me, and gave himself for me'. (Almost one detects a whisper of, 'What a great sinner am I!) The truth is that most of those prepared to say that they find Paul unattractive tend to offer reasons drawn from the pastorals, while others confess to some relief at the suggestion that perhaps it is not Paul himself here dictating.

- (*vii*) *Paul's style, also, seems to have changed greatly.* The obvious disjointedness of the pastorals, especially the letters to Timothy, is not quite like that which makes us suspect composition in *1 Corinthians, Philippians*. There, words like 'finally', or complete change of tone and content, serve to warn us that separate messages may have been copied together; but in the pastorals a constant and abrupt change of subject makes it difficult to follow Paul's thought; and continual repetition adds to the difficulty, even to the tedium. Paul seems to have lost his fluency and literary skill. And, if one dare suggest it, his lucidity. For the pastorals contain the one passage from Paul, according to tradition, of which no one can decipher any meaning — any meaning, that is, consistent with Paul's teaching elsewhere. 1 Timothy 2:11–15 appears to imply that Christian worship is determined by what happened in Eden, not on the cross; that Christ did not undo this part, at any rate, of the ancient curse; that to be deceived makes sinning worse than committing it deliberately; that there is another means of salvation than faith in Christ, namely childbearing, presumably for married women; and that Paul was wrong, after all, in saying that 'In Christ there is neither... male nor female...' It is a *most* perplexing passage!

Much expertise has been expended upon the vocabulary, sentence-structure, conjunctions, prepositions, and other particles in the phrasing of the pastorals, comparing with letters believed to be Paul's in order to prove or disprove his authorship.

The facts are odd, certainly, though somewhat elusive, for different experts count different things, reaching totals ranging from 171 to 306 words, phrases, and the like found in these letters and *nowhere else* in Paul's writings.

Particular (Greek) keywords like piety, sobriety, godliness, sound doctrine, faithful saying, exercise thyself, acceptable, purity, without controversy, accusation, love of money, deposit, found mercy, needing not to be ashamed, lovers of self, and even 'Christ Jesus our saviour' are in this list.

Paul often surprises us with new words and phrases, and in earlier epistles these occur on average once in four-and-a-half verses; in the pastorals new words or phrases occur once in every one and a half verses. The very least that this implies is a new secretary with far greater freedom of expression than former ones.

But more is to be said. Many of Paul's ideas are here found in different words, while many of his favourite phrases are missing ('in Christ', which Paul used hundreds of times, 'body of Christ', 'gifts of the Spirit', 'the God and Father of our Lord Jesus Christ' are but a few). So are some of Paul's most familiar thoughts, as of Christian joy, baptism, the Lord's Supper, dying with Christ, being counted righteous by faith, boasting only in Christ, and the great affirmations concerning the person of Christ, the Spirit, the supremacy of love.

Not all of these differences between the pastorals and the earlier Paul can be explained by change of secretary: *the dictating mind* seems to think in new terms, with different ideas — so different in thought and phrasing as to rule out deliberate imitation, too. A devoted disciple, perhaps, would take care not to contradict his master's teaching, while unable to reproduce his freshness, vigour, and creativeness.

Authorship Theories

All seven of these disturbing impressions, made by the letters themselves, leave hesitations in one's mind about who penned the pastorals. And one further, serious difficulty has to be mentioned. This is the difficulty, or impossibility, of finding place for the events and movements alluded to in the apostle's known story — admittedly incomplete, but even what we know is hard to reconcile with the pastorals.

When did Paul, on the way to Macedonia, leave Timothy at Ephesus? Acts 19:22 says Timothy went ahead; Acts 20 speaks of division and heresy as still future, some years after the Ephesian mission was ended. As far as we know, Paul did not revisit Ephesus as promised in 1 Timothy 3:14.

Paul expects imminent martyrdom in 2 Timothy 4:6, but asks Timothy to come before winter in 4:9,21. Only Luke is with Paul in 2 Timothy 4:11, yet four others, and 'all the brethren' send greetings. Paul sends for cloak, books and parchments he left at Troas, and mentions sick Trophimus, at least six years after leaving them! (If 2 Timothy 4:13,20, 1:17 are meant to trace Paul's journey to Rome, the contrast with Luke's account could not be greater.)

Again, when did Paul evangelize 'every town' on Crete, leaving Titus 'behind' (literally)? If from Corinth, 280 kilometres across the sea, Luke says nothing of it. When did Paul, a free man, winter at Nicopolis on the south-western shores of Greece. Titus did not stay as bidden at Crete, or at Nicopolis, but went to Rome, and thence to Dalmatia (2 Timothy 4:10); of Christian work there we know nothing.

Full explanation being impossible, conjecture is unavoidable. The traditional, widespread, and persistent assumption has been that Paul was released from the house arrest of Acts 28, toured Ephesus, Macedonia, Miletus, Troas, Crete, Nicopolis (as the pastorals seem to presuppose), and possibly Spain (since he so intended); was rearrested, taken to Rome, wrote the pastorals, and perhaps *Philippians* if not all the 'prison epistles', and died about AD 64–65. This hypothesis provides background to the pastorals, and some four to five years longer for changes in atmosphere and organization, and in Paul, to occur.

It is pure invention, of course, in direct contradiction of Paul's announced conviction and plans about his work in the east being ended (Acts 19:21, Romans 15:17–24). Luke knew nothing of it when he published *Acts*, allowing 20:25,38 (saying Paul would visit Ephesus no more) to stand uncorrected, and omitting Rome's verdict from his list of Paul's significant acquittals.

Nor does Paul in the pastorals mention his supposed earlier suffering at Rome, or the massacre of Christians there in AD 64, when asking prayers for the authorities. 'At my first defence' and the vision that followed (2 Timothy 4:16–17) well describes Paul's experience in Jerusalem; the 'desertion' he speaks of would then be by the Jerusalem leaders, not by his own party, who send greetings.

Early Christian historians know nothing of Paul's release and rearrest.

Clement's phrase about Paul preaching 'to the boundaries of the west' is held to mean 'to Rome'; like a few later and equally ambiguous allusions it proves nothing, but could not in any case imply further work in the east. The whole conjectural extension of Paul's career is more daring than helpful, even with the purely historical difficulty.

Another equally radical conjecture, likewise unsupported in the manuscripts and early histories, is that a disciple or admirer of Paul (possibly Timothy himself, and Titus), sensing the decline in the church's thought and conduct, resolved to recall Christians to his standards and principles by reissuing the notes they had received *at different times* from the apostle. Thus they would speak for him such warnings and counsel as they believed Paul would give were he still alive; and so they would feel obliged to use his name and not their own.

This hypothesis would allow a much later date for the changes observed in the church's organization and spiritual temperature, perhaps towards the end of the first century. It would 'explain' too the disjointedness, the 'unPauline' words and style, and a feeling that many have in reading the pastorals, that we are hearing Paul at secondhand, without the vigorous thought and power of inspiration that we expect of him.

Almost the only *argument* that can be raised against this 'explanation' of the pastorals (apart from merely calling it 'fanciful'), is that no Christian would 'ever be guilty of so deceitful a fraud'. But the list of books and fragments in the 'Apocryphal New Testament' leaves no doubt that Christians *did* issue books in the names of apostles, and without any sense of guilt!

Attempts have been made to isolate passages in the pastorals which have 'an authentic Pauline tone', or which can be assigned as separate fragments to various periods in Paul's career, and to treat them as treasured notes now incorporated in later compositions. But the basis of such selection is too subjective to yield much assurance. As a whole the theory seems too convenient: what we happen to like in the pastorals is truly Paul's; what we dislike we can disregard as 'secondary', that is, someone else's.

Certainly the church accepted the pastorals as Paul's — eventually. The earliest existing manuscript of Paul's letters does not contain the pastorals (the manuscript is incomplete, but scholars are convinced it never had room for another 13 chapters). A mid-second-century list of New Testament books omits them, too; and the end-second-century list has them in an unexpected position, 'as though the pastorals were only just being accepted?'

Echoes of language similar to that of the pastorals may be heard in Clement of Rome (about AD 95) and in Polycarp; that might show the date at which the pastorals were written. The letters are too brief and personal to be quoted, some say; yet their relevance to church problems might be expected to keep them before the church's mind. Once again, discussion remains inconclusive.

Continuing Value

With alternatives so insubstantial it is small wonder that many cling to the opinion that Paul wrote the pastorals, taking refuge from the admitted difficulties in the confession of ignorance. *Any* dogmatism is obviously unjustified; and certainty is unattainable. Yet, so long as they are used only with caution when appealed to for 'facts', or for illustration of Paul's teaching or character, the three pastoral letters continue to have real value, especially as 'Christianity according to the pastorals' is so much nearer to the Christianity we know and practise.

The church did, in fact, adopt the cautions, the enquiries, and the training, recommended in the pastorals for its leaders; and has continued to be watchful for the temptations involved in the special privileges and opportunities of the Christian ministry.

But further: the pastoral letters illumine problems that arose as the apostolic age receded into memory. Like those 'sub-apostolic' readers, many today will treasure the glimpses which the pastorals afford of Paul's attitude to his early days, and to his death; of Timothy's background and story; and of the beginnings of a new stage in the church's development. Others point to the practical wisdom, the accumulation of experience, the guide-lines for future organization, all necessary if Christianity was to become 'a working religion for ordinary men', and not the preserve of enthusiasts.

Attempts at various times in church history to return to the high inspiration, the emotional richness, and the variety, the freedom, of the earliest years, illustrate how often Christians have felt and regretted the loss, to which the pastorals bear witness, of Christianity's original drive, resilience, and joy.

Such spiritual nostalgia for the days when the tides of the Spirit were at the full is understandable: it must be preserved. But the church must also face periods of pedestrian pilgrimage through unfavourable times, when only memory, tradition, discipline, and a determined holding fast to what we have learned, will save the church and serve the age. Then, the pastoral epistles, in their turn, speak again, with immediate relevance if not with power.

Suggestions for Group Discussion

1 The qualifications required of church leaders are, in the Pastoral letters, concerned much more with character, and with the temptations inherent in the office, than with right belief or personal gifts. Does the group agree that, in our day of moral weakness *and* intellectual confusion, the same emphasis in choosing our leaders should be paramount?

2 The contrast drawn here between the life of the church in the earliest years — exuberant, free, effervescent, 'gifted', wonderfully varied and spontaneous, and the church-life described in the Pastoral letters — ordered, selective, trained, disciplined, regulated, credal, firmly ruled, faces the church still, both at home and especially abroad, in 'free', 'charismatic', 'house-church' movements, and the like. *Both* types, obviously, are scriptural: which is the pattern for the coming years?

3 Leaving aside the unsettled question of authorship of the Pastoral letters, does the group agree that the Paul represented in these letters is less attractive than the Paul described elsewhere?

4 Since the question of authorship of the Pastorals *is* unsettled (and admitting that much of the argument is somewhat technical), is the group persuaded that Paul did, or did not, write these letters?

CHAPTER 13

Pauline Christianity

Preparatory Reading: (Salvation) Romans 6, 7, 10:8–13;
(Church) Romans 9–11, Ephesians 2:11–22, 4:1–16;
(the Spirit) 1 Corinthians 12–14, Romans 8:1–17

'I delivered to you as of first importance what I also received . . . Whether then it was I or they, so we preach and so you believed'. Paul never forgot, or obscured, his indebtedness to those who were 'in Christ' before him, for his knowledge of Christ's life, teaching, death, and resurrection, for the sacraments, the gospel, the Christian understanding of the Old Testament, the existence of the church into which he came and which commissioned his own ministry. He would repudiate vigorously any suggestion of a 'Pauline Christianity', except as describing a particular *approach* to the common Christian faith, and a particular *emphasis* in propagating it. Yet few mature Christians would fail to recognize that a given verse or passage from the New Testament 'sounds like Paul', as expressing his characteristic outlook and teaching.

For example, to Paul, Christianity was first, last, and essentially a personal *experience*. Its beginning at Damascus was not so unprepared as we sometimes suppose, but it was still an unmistakable climax, a moment of truth and insight amounting to divine revelation, in which things half perceived before became suddenly clear as the daylight, never again to be questioned.

For some, faith is the result of a long search for truth; for others, the fruit of confrontation with the living church; for yet others, it is the natural tendency of a mind that inherited a Christian tradition and culture. For Paul at Damascus — as for Augustine in the garden, for Luther in his cell, for Bunyan in the village street, for Wesley in a devotional meeting — the crucial moment was the intervention of Christ, in a transcendent and transforming experience within his own mind and heart.

And as it began, so Christianity continued to be, for Paul, an inward certainty, power, freedom, resource, guidance, and joy, that nothing could take from him. Inevitably, therefore, one feature of Pauline Christianity is the devout introspection which analyzes that Christian experience, identifying the movements of conviction, faith, assurance, dedication, aspiration, within

124

the Christian soul. Paul is the first of all Christian psychologists, the pioneer exponent of 'the inner life'.

The Psychology of Salvation

The source and foundation of Christian experience remained, for Paul, the objective historical action of God in 'setting forth Christ', in Christ's 'giving himself' for Paul, in God's sending 'the Spirit of his Son' into Christian hearts. Christianity was no mere system of thought, mystical experience, or emotional 'trip'. As in Judaism so in Christianity, divine revelation came through *history*, especially (for Paul) through the appearing, life, ministry, death, and resurrection of Jesus the Christ. Yet in 'faith' each objective historic event became also an inward subjective experience; 'faith' does not merely believe that these events happened, it enters into them and shares their significance.

Certainly Paul saw Jesus through the glory of the Damascus road, and his faith was ever focused upon the risen, ever-living Christ. But it was the historic Jesus whom he saw, heard, believed in — there was no other. And so believing, he became personally, intimately, by a profound empathy, identified with Christ.

That is why, when Paul discusses the dignity of Christ (in *Colossians*), the coming advent of Christ (*Thessalonians*), the Spirit, the Lord's Supper, the resurrection (*1 Corinthians*), the divine purpose (*Ephesians*), God's saving mercies (*Romans*), or Christian freedom (*Galatians*), his last word every time concerns the significance of the doctrine for the daily life and behaviour of the Christian. So the 'mind of Christ' in 'emptying himself' to become incarnate must be reproduced in our selfless concern for others (Philippians 2). The life and character of Jesus become the 'image' to which Christians are to be 'conformed' (Romans 8:29).

Again, the authority of Jesus as teacher is absolute over every Christian's thought and conduct. Paul actually quotes the words of Jesus upon giving (Acts 20:35), divorce (1 Corinthians 7:10–12), support for the ministry (1 Corinthians 9:14), the Lord's Supper (1 Corinthians 11:23–25), and clearly echoes Jesus on love fulfilling the whole law (Romans 13:8–10), the coming advent (1 Thessalonians 5:4,6), and on payment of taxes (Romans 13:5–7).

Someone counted over 1000 'echoes' of Jesus in Paul's writings; if the figure is exaggerated three times, the total remains astonishing when we remember that the gospels were not yet in circulation.

And so, too, with Christ's death and resurrection. If we truly believe that Christ died for our sins we are accepting his verdict that our sinfulness deserves death. We cannot then continue to sin: our sinful nature 'dies' — is 'crucified with him'. We die to sin within, as far as deliberate purpose is concerned, and to the ungodliness in the 'world' about us. Such is the moral realism of Paul's view of faith in the dying Saviour.

We do not say, 'Christ has died, then none need die again'; we say 'one has died for all, therefore all have died. And he died for all that those who live might *live no longer* for themselves but for him who for their sake died and was raised' (2 Corinthians 5:14,15).

Again the historic event has become also an internal experience; Paul is echoing Jesus once more, on our taking up the cross and following him. In the same way, the historic event of Christ's resurrection becomes the pattern of an inward experience for believers: 'if we have been united with him in a death like his, we shall certainly be united with him in a resurrection like his' and 'walk in newness of life', in which neither sin nor death has any longer dominion over us, and we are free to serve God (Romans 6).

We may, if we wish, dismiss this language as mere figure of speech — provided that we do not dismiss the truth Paul is striving to express, for then his psychology of salvation would be reduced to dangerous nonsense. By his faith in the dying and rising Christ the Christian does, in fact, put an end to one way of life and adopt another, as truly if not as dramatically as Paul did on the Damascus road.

We must not forget what Paul was striving to say about forgiveness: that to forgive wrong without condemning it merely condones it, and God is just. The death of Jesus for our sins both condemns sin and cancels it, in the justice and the mercy of God.

Our thought-world is different from Paul's, but the same problems face us, What could God do with sinful men? He could wait until by obeying his law they become good, and then accept them: Paul found in his own life that did not work.

Or: God could accept sinful men as they are, asking only that they want to be good (which is the heart of repentance), and are reaching out for help to become good (which is the moral side of faith). By so accepting the will for the deed, God could help men to *be* good: and that, Paul discovered, does work, and is salvation. But that was too easy, Paul felt, unless men became convinced how wrong sin was, as well as how much God loves. To make both truths perfectly plain, Christ died for our sins.

Doubtless all attempts to explain redemption — deliverance from sin — are unsatisfying. But that Christ did something for us, which was necessary to be done but which we could not do for ourselves, and did it out of love for us to make us different, cannot be eliminated from the gospel. To deny it reduces the Christian message to helpful advice for those already good; in the

126

end it makes Christ redundant, except perhaps for the totally inadequate; and it renders inoperative the overmastering motive of Christian ethics — gratitude for redemption freely given.

According to Paul, the sole condition of that redemption is, that what Christ did for us we shall now let him do in us. Countless devoted, saintly, heroic lives testify that faith in the Christ who died for all does change people, and motivates unlimited dedication. As a theory of redemption, Paul's concepts may be outdated; in experience they work wonders.

And Paul's translation of 'salvation history' into psychological experience goes even further. As we saw in Romans 7 he 'internalizes' the Eden story to illustrate his own journey from childhood innocence through desire for things forbidden to awareness of sin, as Adam had done. We do not sin because Adam sinned, but as he did — 'Every man the Adam of his own soul' (Romans 5:12 — 'because *all men sinned*'). And even Christ's ascension, for Paul unquestionably historical, is also a spiritual experience; we seek 'the things that are above, where Christ is, seated at the right hand of God'. For God has made us 'sit with him in heavenly places' — an orientation of the inner life that transforms the Christian's dullest day!

And once again, if any man be in Christ there is a new *creation* (2 Corinthians 5:17): he finds himself with a renewed nature, new tastes, desires, standards, in a world where all things are made new. Henceforth Christ *is* his 'world': to be 'in Christ' — a phrase which Paul uses 164 times — was to know one's whole inner life organized around the Christ-ideal, one's emotions centred in love for Christ, one's mind as far as possible the mind of Christ, one's will submissive to the lordship of Christ; all ambitions, hopes and desire focused in the aim to please Christ (Colossians 1:10).

Christ was the source of guidance, encouragement, strength, mediated through conscience, prayerful reflection, and 'visions' (whose precise nature it is futile to define). And mostly, Paul spoke of Christ as a personal presence in his life, so that he lived in divine company, 'in fellowship', 'in Christ'.

It is no exaggeration to say that to explore fully what Paul meant by being 'in Christ', one must retell his story and rewrite his correspondence; 'in Christ' is Paul's shorthand for Christian life at its highest and deepest level, touching the entire circumference of experience.

All this, which had to come down to us in archaic-sounding language, was to Paul vivid, exciting, dramatic, and deeply satisfying, daily experience. It is curious that the only parallel, since Augustine to this meticulous dissection of the Christian's inner life is the work of John Bunyan. That flowering of the English Puritan movement sought the secrets of Christian devotion as eagerly as did the best of the pre-Reformation mystics. But all dissection looks back to Paul, and with Paul to Jesus, who in sermon, epigram, and parable, unveiled the human heart, its hopes and fears, its sincerity and shams, its sins and its aspirations, as none other had ever done.

Paul and the Church

Emphasis upon personal religious experience is usually intensely individualistic; with Paul, it is not merely set beside, but almost overshadowed by the central place he gives to the church. The master-builder was essentially a church-builder, his evangelism not only the winning of souls but the creation of communities. Athens might be the one exception: we hear of no congregation there, and no return visit, but that was not by Paul's choice. Everywhere else he left churches. If Paul's Christianity was created by the gospel, it was enshrined within and nourished by the church. That is emphasized nowhere else in the New Testament so strongly and persistently.

Paul's whole mission strategy underlines his confidence in the local church. Even after persecution arose in each centre, he usually stayed long enough to see elders appointed to oversee the new group, or left Timothy, Luke, or Titus to foster the new cause. As we see at Corinth, Paul himself would stay away if unwanted, 'not lording it' over the church, and would leave discipline to be exercised by the local assembly (2 Corinthians 1:23–24, 1 Corinthians 5:3–5). Paul's reliance upon each church to evangelize its own area is highly significant, too; the church, not the evangelist, must develop the work, and may be trusted to do so.

The importance of the church for Paul may be seen even more clearly — given sympathetic insight — in the tremendous wrench involved in his acknowledging the church, this new, varied, multi-racial community of Christian believers scattered far and wide through paganism, to be a *new Israel*. Such an idea was totally repugnant to every Jewish heart. To accept that the church could actually supplant the ancient, divinely-chosen family-nation, with its rich heritage, history, promises and destiny, as the agent of God in bringing blessing to all the nations of the world, was unthinkable.

What the admission cost Paul may be estimated by the tortuous argument of Romans 9–11, where in spite of his own premises, and against all appearances, he clings tenaciously to the hope that the old Israel will yet somehow be included in the new. Meanwhile, Paul does accept the divine choice of the church of many races: 'we are the circumcision' he wrote to the Gentile Philippians; 'the true Jew is he who shares Abraham's faith', he told the Romans; 'Abraham is the father of us all . . . of many nations'.

Hence Paul's constant concern for the welfare, and especially for the unity, of each church. Within the church the man of faith must be a support to fellow Christians, selfless, prayerful, humble, hospitable, while on minor disagreements, individual freedom must yield to loving concern for those who think differently (*Romans*).

The pre-conditions of inter-personal unity are carefully analyzed in Philippians 2, as selflessness, concern for others' interests, recognition of others' superiority, willingness to empty oneself as Christ did, so as to attain 'similar outlook, the same love, one accord, united purpose' and 'stand firm in one mind, one spirit, side by side'.

In *Ephesians* all divisive, selfish, abrasive behaviour is to be excluded; the great offences against mutual respect and confidence — lying, stealing, immorality, evil conversation, slander — are outlawed. Nothing must be allowed to grieve the Spirit indwelling the whole; for Christians are now both integrated within themselves and 'socialized' as fellow-members of the one church Christ loves.

At Corinth, Paul resolutely set his face against partisanship, urging appreciation of all types of leadership, all varied gifts, without comparisons: 'All are yours', enjoy them all! In the same generous spirit he rejoiced that Christ was preached, even by rivals taking advantage of his imprisonment at Ephesus. And to colleagues he is always loyal and appreciative. Plainly the local church's unity was too important to sacrifice to personal aggrandizement.

So was the unity of all the churches; by letters, visits, messengers, reports to Palestine, explaining Gentiles and Jews to each other, Paul strove to keep the separate churches in touch and praying for each other. The collection of Gentile gifts for Judean Christians in need reveals Paul's concern for the unity of the whole people of God. Yet not to *create* unity among unrelated groups, but to express, foster, and deepen the unity already present in the one church, one body indwelt by one Spirit, holding to one Lord, one faith, one baptism, one God and Father of all.

This is the more remarkable in that Paul made no attempt to impose on the different churches any single pattern of worship or government, nor to bring all under the jurisdiction of the church at Jerusalem — as Jerusalem had attempted to do in Samaria and at Syrian Antioch. The unity Paul valued was not of structure, or of uniform practice, but of inner experience, shared ideals, common purpose, mutual recognition and appreciation, within the freedom of the Spirit.

Behind all was Paul's vision of the over-riding purpose of God to reconcile all things in the fragmented universe under one head, namely Christ; and of the church, the one commonwealth, household, temple, people of God, as the firstfruits, the model, and the agency of that universal reconciliation.

The question arises, not quite pointlessly, whether Paul wished most to establish churches so that individuals might hear the gospel and be saved, or to save individuals so that the churches so formed might serve the universal purpose of God. Paul would probably not separate the two motives: but it is certain he would have little interest in the kind of evangelism that feeds statistics, promotes the evangelist, and leaves little that is permanent behind.

For Paul, Christianity was an individual experience of salvation, kindled, nourished, and expressed within the ongoing life of Christ's church.

Paul and the Spirit

In the longest view, probably the most important feature of Pauline Christianity is his illumination of the idea of the Spirit. Christianity inherited this conception from Judaism, as the invisible power of God at work in creation and in Nature, and the source of inspiration of the prophets.

Paul's contribution to Christian understanding of the Spirit lies somewhere between Luke's description of Pentecost, where the Spirit is 'poured out' (or one is 'baptised in' the Spirit), and where the 'signs' of the Spirit, wind, fire, strange speech, point back to the Old Testament (especially to *Joel*); and the maturest reflection in the New Testament in the Gospel of John, where the Spirit is the 'form' of the risen, returning Christ, Christ's 'other self', now 'with' the disciples, soon to be 'in them', leading into all truth, guiding into the future, but with no mention of 'signs and wonders'. Between these milestones, Paul expounded the Christian's experience of the Spirit, both individually and corporately.

In Paul's writings we first meet 'identification' of the Spirit with the risen, indwelling Christ: 'Now the Lord is the Spirit . . . the Spirit of the Lord . . . the Spirit of Christ'. Henceforth the Spirit is no nameless power or 'element' (such as can be 'poured') but a divine person who loves, wills, distributes gifts, bears witness, sanctifies, has 'mind', ushers into the presence of the Father (Romans 8:16,27, 15:30, 1 Corinthians 12:11, Ephesians 2:18). In consequence, the conception of the Spirit's work is moralized. We hear nothing of those 'possessed of the Spirit' lying naked on the hillside, or wielding the jawbone of an ass; even the more spectacular signs witnessed at Pentecost are in Paul's thought given second place.

Paul performed miracles of healing (at Philippi, Troas, Ephesus and elsewhere), and he 'spoke in tongues', and counts these phenomena among 'demonstrations of the Spirit and of power', 'the signs of an apostle'. But in his letters he never recounts these stories, or supplies details. Alone among 'Paul's' churches, that at Corinth, beset with the claims of heathen temples and cults, made much of these 'signs', evidently with some feeling of rivalry towards the pagans. Paul declares the church 'comes behind in no gift', and lists the special manifestations among them without questioning that they are 'of the Spirit'.

130

Yet Paul's own attitude to these 'signs' is clear, though unexpected. He nowhere denigrates these manifestations so as to shake the faith or quench the zeal and assurance of young Corinthian converts. To distinguish the ecstatic 'tongues speaking' claimed by pagan cults with their 'divine oracles' (compare Acts 16:16–20) from the genuine 'gift of the Spirit', Paul offers a clear criterion — confession of the lordship of Christ (1 Corinthians 12:1–3).

Then he firmly requires the Corinthians, in their enthusiasm for such experiences:

(1) To remember that all such 'gifts' are from the same Spirit and given as *he* wills; they offer no ground, therefore, for competition or disparagement among members.

(2) To evaluate the various gifts by their actual usefulness in building up fellow Christians and the church; they should desire the 'best' gifts, which means especially to prophesy (that is, to preach) so as to instruct, exhort, encourage.

Paul would prefer to speak five words in plain Greek than 10,000 in an unknown tongue, which, beside being profitless, would make an incoming stranger think the congregation all 'mad'. Paul actually forbids the public display of 'tongues', gift of the Spirit or no, unless an interpreter is present to give the display meaning.

(3) They must discipline the display of 'gifts', two or three only prophesying in a given meeting, and then one at a time. Twice the command is given 'Be silent!' — Spirit or no Spirit! Being 'possessed by the Spirit' is evidently no excuse for bad manners, while 'the spirits of prophets are subject to prophets', and 'God is not a God of confusion but of peace . . . all things should be done decently and in order.'

(4) The worshippers must 'Weigh what is said' — a remarkable instruction: speaking under claimed inspiration is no guarantee that what is said is true, or wise. The hearer must reflect, and test, as Paul himself did over the 'inspired' prophecy of Agabus (Acts 21:10–14). It is plain that while accepting the phenomena themselves, Paul's thought is steadily moving away from the more spectacular and bizarre 'signs of the Spirit' to emphasize instead what is useful, orderly, intelligible, disciplined, profitable, and morally uplifting.

For in the midst of this discussion Paul pauses upon the 'more excellent way' of demonstrating the presence of the Spirit, more excellent even than speaking with tongues of angels, or prophesying, or understanding divine secrets, and being equipped to teach, exercising faith to remove mountains, giving away all one's possessions, or suffering martyrdom — all of which, in themselves, are 'nothing': better than all, as a sign of the Spirit, is *love*.

This moral aspect of the Spirit's ministry is emphasized in *Romans*, where the Spirit indwelling the believer mortifies the flesh, and imparts divine life within the soul; yielding purity, life, peace, a life led by the Spirit, assured of sonship, assisted intercession, all things being made to work towards conformity to Christ.

Galatians adds the ninefold harvest of the Spirit in the virtues and graces of a Christlike character. Paul's frequently repeated phrase 'holy Spirit' (where 'holy' is an adjective of quality, not a 'Christian name'! compare 'Spirit of holiness' Romans 1:4) has passed into Christian use as a permanent reminder of Paul's moralizing of the conception of the Spirit of God.

Luke fully shares Paul's emphasis upon the Spirit; John shares Paul's view of the Spirit as the Spirit of Christ; but Paul is alone in the New Testament in representing the Spirit as the replacement in Christian life of the sacred law in Old Testament piety.

Both Paul's own experience of the failure of the law to save, and the later Judaist controversy, brought this aspect of truth to the forefront. Christians must not be compelled to observe the Mosaic law — so Paul argued in *Galatians* — in order that they might be free to live and walk under the inspiration of the Spirit. In 2 Corinthians 3, likewise, Paul rejects 'tablets of stone', 'the written code which kills', in favour of 'the dispensation of the Spirit', and for the same reason, because 'where the Spirit of the Lord is, there is liberty'.

In *Romans* Paul argues that what the law could not do, 'the Spirit of life in Christ Jesus' does, and again adds the testimony 'the rule of the Spirit . . . has made me free . . .'. 'Christ is the end of the law'; henceforth inward prompting and constraint towards what is good shall replace outward compulsion and restraint; the new man is ruled from within, *wanting* what he *ought*, which is safe enjoyable freedom, and complete, too, since it releases the religious man from the bondage of law (*Galatians*), and the sinful man from the bondage of an evil nature (*Romans*).

The Spirit, then, in Paul's thought, is not only the Spirit of Christ, and the Spirit of holiness, but the Spirit of liberty also. The 'signs' or 'gifts' of the Spirit Paul would have us look for and covet, in the Christian and in the church, are Christlikeness, love, and liberty.

A Fine Balance

Thus Pauline Christianity has a fine balance of emphasis. While personal experience is the heart of individual religion, it must be set within, and expressed through, Christ's church. While the church is supremely important in the purpose of God, its life and resource lie ultimately in the individual member's experience of Christ. While individual experience and church fellowship are important, and human in context and expression, yet Christianity is essentially supranatural. Or, to avoid overtones of magic and mere spectacle, 'supranatural', as being 'more than natural' but finding expression and outlet through what is natural and human.

Incarnation remains the basic word in Christianity. Certainly, for Paul, Christianity can be analyzed, organized, persecuted, fostered, affected in many ways by human faith, devotion, disloyalty, denial, opposition. Yet it is neither humanist, nor self-redeeming; it is not man's to create, or to destroy. It is the invasion of God into history and human experience, through Christ once, and through the Spirit continually, indwelling the consenting personality and the devoted group, to enhance, uplift, guide, cleanse, sustain. So the Spirit works out purposes beyond human reach and imagining, but ultimately to man's immeasurable good, and God's eternal glory.

So Paul understood Jesus.

Suggestions for Group Discussion

1 'Incarnation remains the basic word in Christianity': let the group consider whether this is the key to (i) the Word of God within a humanly-written Bible; (ii) the holy church of God within the sort of people we actually worship with; (iii) the Holy Spirit within the Christians we have known. Or is it just an excuse for our failures?

2 Paul lays down one clear test of the presence of Christ's Spirit in any individual or church — 1 Corinthians 12:3. Can the group suggest other reliable criteria of the presence of God's Spirit in any leader, movement, or church?

3 Many people feel that Paul has made salvation unnecessarily complicated; others, recalling Romans 6:1, feel that, faced with ideas like 'only believe, it does not matter how you live', Paul had to show how 'saving faith' actually works. Which is right, and does the group think Paul succeeded?

4 Let the group now share, very frankly, its impressions, appreciation, and criticisms, of the apostle Paul.

FURTHER READING

One hundred books about St Paul are currently in print. Two excellent, though very different, older books may be obtainable from libraries:

T. R. Glover: *Paul of Tarsus*

J. S. Stewart: *A Man in Christ*

Also recommended:

William Barclay: *The Mind of St Paul*

C. H. Dodd: *The Meaning of Paul for Today*

F. F. Bruce: *Paul and His Converts*

John Drane: *St Paul*

Donald Coggan: *Paul: Portrait of a Revolutionary*

On separate epistles:

F. F. Bruce: *New Testament Documents*

William Barclay: *Daily Study Bible*

INDEX

INDEX OF SCRIPTURE PASSAGES

The passages here are only those specifically considered in the text.